General Editor
Patrick McNei

Deviance

Other books in the **Society Now** series

Peter Aggleton

DEVIANCE

Tavistock Publications · London · New York

First published in 1987 by
Tavistock Publications Ltd
11 New Fetter Lane,
London EC4P 4EE

© 1987 Peter Aggleton

Set by Hope Services, Abingdon
Printed in Great Britain by
Richard Clay Ltd
Bungay, Suffolk

*British Library Cataloguing
in Publication Data*
Aggleton, Peter
Deviance.— (Society now)
1. Deviant behaviour
I. Title. II. Series
302.5'42 HM291
ISBN 0–422–60480–1

Contents

Preface

People have always been interested in behaviour that is unusual in some way, and social scientists have devoted a great deal of energy to explaining the actions of those who deviate from the norm. They do this not, as popular opinion would have us believe, in order to *excuse* the behaviour they investigate, but in order to *understand* it more fully.

In this book, I try to present, in simple terms, some of the more important explanations of deviance that have been developed by social scientists. These vary in their complexity from those that are very close to 'commonsense' ways of understanding normal and deviant behaviour to those that challenge what we may uncritically believe to be true of ourselves and others. I hope you find the book interesting, and finish reading it with a fuller understanding of the creative aspects of deviance and a greater tolerance towards the social differences that surround you.

I dedicate this book to Julia who helped me recover from writing it, to Andy without whose love and support I would never have begun, and to women and men everywhere who struggle every day to be what they are.

1

The nature of deviance and deviant behaviour

What is deviance? To ask this, is in many ways to challenge what so many people take for granted – the normal state of affairs. Maybe you imagine that there exist certain sorts of behaviour that are 'deviant' and others that are 'normal'. The individuals who display the former deviate from the norm in some way. They make up a deviant minority within society: the rest do not. However, when it comes to specifying the qualities that supposedly 'normal' and 'deviant' people possess, things become less clear cut than such commonsense understandings would have us believe. Sociologists, in particular, have puzzled long and hard about the issue of deviance and it is in order to introduce you to some of their conclusions that this book has been written.

To help explore the concept of deviance more fully, it may be helpful to identify a few examples of behaviour which could be considered deviant and to think about these a little more critically. In a recent book about deviance, Douglas (1984) has identified rape, homosexuality and terrorism as major categories of deviance today, and his choice of these highlights a recurrent concern among sociologists to link an analysis of deviance with that of particular forms of sexual and violent behaviour. Indeed, a quick glance through the contents of any book dealing with deviance is likely to reveal an interest in making sense of forms of sexual behaviour as diverse as prostitution, child abuse, homosexuality, transsexualism and extra-marital sexual activity. Similarly, with respect to violence, interest has been shown in gang violence, rape, juvenile delinquency, football hooliganism and acts of terrorism. To this list of concerns, however, should be added studies looking at less spectacular forms of deviance such as alcohol dependence, childlessness, stuttering, and solvent use.

In investigating and explaining such forms of behaviour, sociologists have encountered a variety of difficulties. Some of these have related to the difficulty of defining what we mean by deviance. Others have been connected with problems to do with measuring how much deviance there is. Additionally, since there are many different theories that try to explain deviant behaviour, deciding between these has created a further set of dilemmas for social scientists.

Before we can begin to appreciate more fully the nature of deviance and deviant behaviour, it is helpful to have a clearer idea of what exactly it is that we want to understand. Sociologists have identified a number of somewhat different approaches to deciding what deviance is but, broadly speaking, these can be classified under two headings: *absolute* and *relative* approaches to defining deviance.

Absolute approaches to defining deviance

Until the early 1950s, many sociologists believed that there were certain forms of behaviour that were deviant regardless of the context in which they occurred. Those who committed them (the deviants in society) were abnormal in some way and differed considerably in their actions from other members of the population. This approach to deviance, which argues that certain actions are universally and absolutely deviant because they break fundamental expectations about human behaviour, is what we call an *absolute* approach to defining deviance.

Activities

1 Make a list of six types of people that you consider to be deviant in all cultures and at all times in history.
2 Working in groups of three or four, compare your list with that of others and see if you agree.

Problems exist with this approach, however, as soon as we try to identify what such universally deviant behaviours might be. To take an extreme case, perhaps you imagined that killing another person is a universally deviant activity. However, anthropological research among eskimo communities at the turn of the present century suggests that infanticide, senilicide and invalidicide (the killing of young children, the elderly, and those who are sick, respectively), were common and socially acceptable practices.

'A hunter living on the Diomede Islands related to the writer how he killed his own father, at the latter's request. The old eskimo was failing, he could no longer contribute what he thought would be his share as a member of the group; so he asked his son, then a lad about twelve years old, to sharpen a big hunting knife. Then he indicated the vulnerable spot over his heart where his son should stab him. The boy plunged the knife deep, but the stroke failed to take effect. The old father suggested with dignity and resignation, "Try a little harder my son". The second stab was effective, and the patriarch passed into the realm of the ancestral shades.'

(Weyer 1924:138)

3

In the light of this evidence, it is necessary to consider whether acts that may seem unusual, and perhaps immoral, to us are intrinsically and absolutely deviant. Such issues can, to some extent, be resolved if we make a distinction between actions and behaviours that break the law (as the above type of behaviour would in many societies today), and others which simply go against expectations or standardized ways of acting. The infringement of expectations of norms we can call *deviance*, the breaking of laws we can call *crime*.

Of course, it is not always possible to distinguish between crime and deviance as clearly as this. Some actions may simultaneously break social norms and criminal laws. In many societies, infanticide and senilicide would be good examples of this type of behaviour. Other actions such as driving at speeds above the official limit or smoking marijuana, infringe laws but may still be consistent with community norms. Other behaviours may simply deviate from dominant sets of expectations. For example, it has been estimated that nearly 3% of the population in Britain today is vegetarian (Gallup Poll 1985). Such individuals constitute a small, but significant, group of people who infringe dominant expectations about dietary preference.

Because of these observations, care needs to be taken in distinguishing criminal acts from those which are deviant, while not forgetting that these may not always be exclusive categories.

Recognizing that norms vary from society to society, and from time to time in history, has created major problems for absolute approaches to deviance. To argue, for example, that vegetarianism is intrinsically and universally deviant makes little sense. After all, among orthodox Hindu communities, eating meat is a deviant act. Problems such as these have therefore led many sociologists to reject absolute approaches in favour of more relative ones.

Relative approaches to defining deviance

Two sorts of study have been particularly influential in

encouraging a move in recent years to more relative definitions of deviance. Findings from research which compares sex-role socialization in different cultures, as well as historical research exploring changes in patterns of sexual behaviour over time have, in particular, raised important questions about the existence (or otherwise) of universal patterns of human behaviour against which deviant actions can be contrasted.

With respect to research exploring cross-cultural differences in sex-role behaviour, studies by anthropologists such as Phillis Kaberry and Margaret Mead have suggested that patterns of work, both inside and outside the home, vary widely across cultures. Kaberry (1952), for example, discovered that among the Bamenda in Africa women do all the agricultural work because it is 'well known' that women are stronger than men. To illustrate the existence of such views, she cites the example of a group of men talking about a wifeless neighbour: 'He works hard; indeed, he works almost as hard as a woman.'

Mead's (1976) work too, although recently criticized on the grounds that it misrepresented life in some of the societies she studied (Freeman 1984), raises questions about the universal nature of norms governing sex-role behaviour. Indeed, by standards prevalent in American society at the time she was writing, Mead was able to identify a wide variety of different patterns of behaviour among those living in different parts of New Guinea. Among the people of the Tchambuli, for example, women adopted behavioural patterns typical of American males, and males adopted those more characteristic of American females.

Social historians too have played an important role in challenging those who argue for the existence of universally shared norms in the field of sexual practice. Bullough (1976), for example, has argued that attitudes to homosexual behaviour among men vary widely throughout history. In classical Greece, for example, it was expected that from about the age of sixteen, throughout the period of military training,

5

and from a brief time thereafter until rights of citizenship were granted, younger men would enter into homosexual relationships with older males. Thereafter, for some years a predominantly heterosexual lifestyle would be entered into, involving marriage and having children. Later in life, the man concerned would be likely to take a younger boy under his custody and the cycle would be repeated. Similarly, positive references to homo-erotic love are to be found in the writings of Roman authors such as Virgil, Horace and Catullus, although the relevant passages are rarely studied in schools and colleges today.

Even today, attitudes to homosexuality vary widely within and between cultures. The age of consent for homosexual relations gives some indication of these differences in attitudes. For men, this varies from fifteen in France and Poland, twenty-one in the United Kingdom (subject to certain provisos about the location of the activities concerned and the employment of the individuals involved) to the situation in certain parts of the United States and in the Soviet Union where such behaviour is currently illegal at any age. Similar patterns of variation exist with respect to homosexual behaviour among women. If actions that are frowned upon in one culture can be positively accepted in others, this would seem to call into question the value of absolute definitions of deviance.

Having said this, if we work with more *relative* approaches, we need to take great care to clearly identify the standards against which particular actions and behaviours are to be judged in deciding whether or not they constitute acts of deviance. Broadly speaking, sociologists have adopted two, rather different, approaches in doing this. The first of these defines as deviant, actions which are *statistically uncommon*. The second approach defines as deviant, behaviours which *run contrary to norms* existing in the society, group or community in which the behaviour occurs.

Deviance as statistically uncommon behaviour

Defining deviance as behaviour that is statistically rare is an approach which, at first sight, seems to have some value. However, when we come to examine the types of behaviour which such an approach would identify as deviant, problems begin to occur. For example, according to such a definition, those who drink hot chocolate, those who never drop litter in the street, as well as those who attend a place of worship without fail each week, could all be classed as deviant. Similarly, among vegetarians, vegans (those who avoid all animal products including milk, eggs and cheese) would be a deviant minority. Obviously, since so many routine and everyday behaviours would have to be classified as deviant using this approach, it would seem to be of limited value.

Deviance as undesirable norm-breaking behaviour

On the other hand, we could define deviance as behaviour which violates certain widely shared expectations or norms. However, this type of analysis encounters problems too, as soon as questions are asked about *what* these widely shared norms are, *who* holds them and *where* they come from. Clearly, there exist few values that are universally shared throughout society. Moreover, norms governing behaviour in one situation may not apply in another. Consider the case of a young person who turns up for his or her first day's work as an office cleaner in a smart business outfit. Such behaviour would be likely to be norm-violating within this particular context, as the individual concerned might very quickly find out. Yet the same behaviour could be entirely appropriate, perhaps, for employees in the office of a prestigious insurance company. Indeed, turning up for work in more casual clothing in this context might be regarded as a sign of deviance. It would seem, therefore, that norms governing behaviour vary widely from situation to situation *within* a culture as well as between cultures.

In order to get around difficulties such as this, some sociologists have found the concept of *subculture* a useful one. According to Sebald, whereas 'culture refers to a blueprint for behaviour of a total society, the largest human grouping, subculture refers to the blueprint for behaviour of a smaller group within society' (Sebald 1968:230). It may therefore be possible to see society as consisting of a large number of separate but interrelated subcultures. These might include those created by household groups, work groups, leisure groups and so on; each with their own norms, contravention of which constitutes deviance. Such an image of society is, in many ways, a useful one, since it opens up the possibility that different subcultural norms can conflict with one another. Those operating within the home, for example, may not match those at school or at work. This sort of conflict can be seen in the case of those whose families exert pressure on them to marry someone who is chosen by the parents, but who themselves spend much of their time among peers who believe that marriage should take place only after a romantic interlude involving courtship and love. Such people might experience a particularly acute set of tensions between competing sets of expectations. Conflicts between norms, therefore, can have very real consequences for the nature of people's lives.

Furthermore, the existence of such tensions can shed light on the processes by which some individuals come to be defined as deviant and others are not. In particular, sociologists such as Howard Becker (1963) and Edwin Lemert (1967) have argued that actions and behaviours become identified as deviant through a process of *labelling*. According to these writers, a deviant person is simply someone to whom the label 'deviant' has been successfully applied. Labelling is, however, rarely an uncontested process. People struggle to reject the labels others put on them or the connotations of these. For example, many an argument takes place in schools today over the efforts of some teachers to ensure that school uniform is worn. Failure to comply with teachers' wishes can, in some cases, result in attempts being made to label the student concerned as 'delinquent' or 'troublesome' in some way – an identification often rejected by the person in question. Likewise, in England, may women teachers have struggled for, and won, the right to wear trousers at their place of work – behaviour originally perceived as deviant by many male teachers working within the same context.

Deviance and power

Conflicts such as these show that the process of being labelled deviant is one which involves the use of *power*. Some groups, however, are more powerful than others in making their interpretation of a situation seem 'right' and 'reasonable'. Hence, if a doctor labels you as neurotic or depressed, the consequences are likely to be more serious for you than if your best friend calls you this as a joke. Similarly, some groups may be more able to escape the attempted imposition of labels than others. Types of property destruction such as window breaking or the writing of graffiti on walls are more likely to be successfully labelled as instances of 'vandalism' (a deviant type of behaviour in the eyes of many) when carried out by young people living in an inner city area than when committed by the undergraduates of, say, an Oxford college. Here, such behaviour is more likely to be viewed as 'high spirits' and 'youthful exuberance', particularly when the actions concerned are committed by the sons and daughters of powerful politicians or wealthy industrialists. Howard and Barbara Myerhoff's (1964) studies of middle class youth in Los Angeles confirm such suggestions. They cite occasions when the behaviour of the middle-class high school students they were studying was clearly such as to cause offence to others. On one occasion, a group of such boys were observed driving slowly up and down the main shopping street spraying well-dressed shoppers with fire extinguishers. Yet official disapproval of this action was mild to say the least, the

9

behaviour in question being interpreted by the police as requiring little more than a quiet talking to.

The idea that the successful labelling of others as deviant must involve the use of power is one which also finds support in the work of Edwin Schur who claims that,

> 'Deviance is not a property *inherent* in certain forms of behaviour, it is a property *conferred upon* these forms by the audiences who directly or indirectly witness them. Sociologically, then, the critical variable is the social audience since it is the audience which eventually decides whether or not any given action or actions will become a visible case of deviation.'
>
> (Schur 1971:43)

Many sociologists have found this a useful approach to understanding deviance since it directs attention away from so-called 'deviant' behaviours to the processes by which particular actions become *defined as deviant*. Moreover, by alerting us to the role played by power in the process of defining behaviours as deviant, relative analyses such as these, enable better sense to be made of the origins and effects of the labelling process itself.

Activities

1 Without looking back at earlier parts of this chapter, try to identify three problems associated with absolute definitions of deviance.
2 Make a list of groups of people that you think would be relatively powerless to resist being labelled as deviant. Then make a list of those who have the power to label these as such. In groups of three or four, or as a class, select three of these groups and try to identify some of the ways in which their members might try to resist being labelled as deviant.

Explaining deviance

At this point, it is useful to move from an examination of the different ways in which deviance has been defined to look at the different kinds of explanation that sociologists have offered for it. To some extent we have begun this task already, since underpinning the different definitions of deviance we have met are particular assumptions about its nature and causes. For example, if we define deviance as an absolute quality inherent in certain acts, we set it up as an identifiable and perhaps measurable 'thing' existing within individuals and their behaviour.

On the other hand, if we believe that deviance is better understood as the outcome of a labelling process, our object of study might become, not so much the behaviour in question and the person exhibiting it, as the social relationships involved in the labelling process itself.

Implicit within the various definitions of deviance we have looked at, therefore, are particular theories about the causes of deviance. In the final part of this chapter, it is useful to identify in general terms the range of theories of deviance that exist. In the rest of this book, each of these approaches will be examined more fully.

Broadly speaking, we can distinguish two major perspectives on deviance: those which see it as a set of behaviours *inherent*, for whatever reason, in persons or groups; and those which see it as the *outcome of processes of interaction*. Within these two broad types of explanation, however, there exist more specific accounts of deviant behaviour. Theories falling within the former of these perspectives include what have been referred to as *biological-, psychological-* and *social-positivist* explanations of deviance. Theories relating to the latter approach include *interactionist* and *structural* accounts of deviant behaviour.

Biological-, psychological- and social-positivist explanations of deviance

In sociology in general, *positivist* theories are those which argue that the methods and techniques that have been used to study the physical world can be used with equal success in making sense of social behaviour. By careful measurement, and by the rigorous use of scientific method, positivist sociologists try to discover law-like generalities relating to human behaviour. August Comte, who died in 1857, was an early researcher of this persuasion. He spent much of his life trying to make sociology a 'positive science of society' by using scientific method to study social phenomena – hence the term 'positivist' to describe this type of activity.

Within a positivist approach to the study of deviance, the first thing to be done is to distinguish deviant from so-called normal behaviour. For many (but not all) positivist analyses this is a relatively simple task, since deviant actions are those which break the law. Many positivist analyses of deviance, particularly early ones, worked from the assumption that crime and deviance could in most cases be considered the same thing. Having identified a suitable topic for investigation, positivist researchers turn their attention to studying the factors that accompany deviant behaviour in the hope that some of these will subsequently be identifiable as *causes* of deviance.

In some positivist accounts, biological factors are focused upon. In the cruder theories of this type, the presence of particular anatomical characteristics such as large ears, high cheek bones, extra fingers and so on, has been associated with tendencies towards deviance. In more sophisticated explanations, 'higher order' biological factors are emphasized as causes of deviant behaviour. These have included the presence or absence of certain chromosomes, the existence of particular hormonal disturbances and, more recently, the overall level of physiological arousal within a person.

A number of these theories have tried to link the biological condition of a person to their psychological state, arguing perhaps that biology can influence the human ability to learn effectively from past experience. Hence, some individuals may be more prone than others to committing acts that are socially disapproved of. *Biological-positivist* and *psychological-positivist* accounts of deviance such as these will be examined more fully in Chapter 2 of this book.

Other positivist explanations of deviance have focused more specifically on social factors that might cause deviant behaviour. In these, particular patterns of socialization within the home, school or peer group may be identified as causes of deviance. Alternatively, aspects of neighbourhood or community structure may be said to encourage the development of deviant behaviour. *Social-positivist* theories of deviance will be looked at in detail in Chapter 3.

Interactionist and structural explanations of deviance

Were we to reject absolute notions of deviance and the positivist explanations that they imply, and focus more specifically on definitions of deviance which emphasize its social relativity, somewhat different explanations seem more appropriate. In particular, if we believe that deviance is basically a label attributed to behaviour, we might want to explore more thoroughly how the labelling of deviant behaviour takes place. By doing this, it might be possible to understand more fully how deviant identities come to be constructed, what meanings these have for those concerned and how they come to be reproduced in particular situations and circumstances. Such *interactionist* accounts of deviance will be explored more fully in Chapter 4.

It may, however, be possible to take explanations such as these one step further if we believe that the power which individuals exert over others is associated with the position they occupy in the social structure of society as a whole. By introducing the idea that the likelihood of being labelled as deviant may vary with the social class, the gender, the age and the ethnicity of the person labelled – as well as with that of the person attempting the labelling – we can begin to build what are sometimes called *structural* explanations of deviance. These will be discussed in Chapter 5.

These major approaches to explaining deviance are summarized in *Table 1*.

Table 1   *A summary of approaches to defining and explaining deviance*

Type of definition	absolute (Certain acts are inherently deviant)		relative (Deviance is socially defined)	
Type of explanation	Biological- and psychological-positivist	Social-positivist	Interactionist	Structural

Activities

1 **Without looking back through this chapter, make a list of the main features associated with biological- positivist-, social-positivist, interactionist and structural approaches to the study of deviance. After you have done this, check back through the material you have read to make sure that the points you have made are similar to those you have read about.**

2

Biological-, psychological- and early social-positivist theories of deviance

In the first chapter, a distinction was drawn between positivist explanations of deviance which are biological and psychological in their emphasis and those which are more socially inclined. All of these types of explanation, however, argue that by following the methods of the natural sciences, social scientists can find clearly identifiable *causes* of deviance. Biological- and psychological-positivist explanations argue that the causes of deviant behaviour, in the sense of norm-breaking, are to be found largely within individuals; in their genetic make-up, their personality or their learned behaviour. Social-positivist explanations, on the other hand, acknowledge that the origins of deviant behaviour may be external to people; residing perhaps in the households, communities and neighbourhoods of which they are a part. In this chapter, we shall look at both of these types of explanation. First, a number of positivist explanations of deviance with biological and psychological emphases will be examined. After this, we shall begin our exploration of social-positivist explanations of deviance by looking at the work of a group of researchers at the University of Chicago in the 1920s who devised what have been called *social ecological* explanations of deviance. A more extended discussion of other types of social-positivist explanation will take place in Chapter 3.

Before we do this, however, it is important to realize that most early biological- and early social-positivist explanations of deviance focused on forms of behaviour which were both *deviant* and *criminal*. This is significant because it means that they were developed to explain a relatively small range of deviant behaviours – those which simultaneously break norms and laws. As we shall see later, this focus is rather different from that adopted by more recent explanations of deviance.

The origins of biological explanations of deviance

Until the late 1700s, explanations of deviance in the sense of norm-breaking fell into two main types. The first approach, one widely held among Western societies under the influence of the Christian church, argued that deviant behaviour was the result of either demonic possession or moral depravity. A second, and somewhat earlier, type of explanation maintained that deviant behaviour resulted from an overall imbalance between four bodily humours: blood, mucus, yellow bile and black bile. Diseases, bad temperaments and immoral lifestyles were all held to be the effects of imbalance between these different bodily humours. Throughout the middle ages, the influence of these ideas was considerable, and people who nowadays might be diagnosed as, perhaps, physically and mentally ill would then have probably been the recipients of 'theological' interventions, such as ordeals by fire and water, and 'medical' treatments, such as purging and blood letting, in efforts to make their behaviour more acceptable.

While there is some tension between these rather different early explanations of deviant behaviour, they all emphasize the presence of something within the individual as the primary cause of deviant behaviour. Similar ideas can also be found in the work of writers such as Benjamin Rush who, as a physician and friend of the Pilgrim Fathers (1620), is often regarded as one of the founders of modern American psychiatry. Rush believed that there was little difference between mental and bodily diseases, and argued that alcoholism, lying, smoking, and suicide, as well as theft and murder, were all evidence of mental disorders arising from bodily illness. His ideas subsequently led to the development of a wide range of medical 'remedies' for deviant behaviour, many of which involved the swallowing of obnoxious substances which, it was said, would cure the underlying illness. Others involved the use of deprivation, solitary confinement and enforced stillness through the use of the straitjacket, in efforts to 'cure' people of their deviance. These new approaches emphasized the need for specialist expertise to identify the slightest sign or symptom of pathology within the individual. In consequence, the nineteenth century saw a resurgence of interest in arts such as *physiognomy*, *metoposcopy* and *phrenology*, all of which attempted to predict, from bodily and facial features and from the shape of the skull, the character of the individual.

In a series of essays published in 1789, Johan Lavater had originally claimed that personality characteristics, such as friendliness, aggression and honesty, could be discerned from a close examination of the shape of the head. Towards the end of the nineteenth century, such ideas were taken up in the work of the Italian researcher, Cesare Lombroso. After some time studying crime and deviance among animals and even plants(!), Lombroso turned his attention to human beings. After carrying out research in prisons and asylums, he concluded that features such as jaw size, abnormal dentition, facial asymmetry, and large ears, as well as the presence of extra fingers, toes and nipples, could all be related to deviant and criminal behaviour. Alcoholism, sexual deviance and mental illness, as well as behaviour which led to breaking the

17

law, came therefore to be explained quite straightforwardly in terms of physical characteristics.

Similar ideas also informed the work of one of Lombroso's colleagues, Enrico Ferri, who extended these arguments to suggest that factors other than those of a purely biological nature might have a role to play in causing deviance. In particular, he claimed that physical factors connected with the climate, the seasons of the year and the time of day, etc., as well as social factors to do with population density, customs and values, could also affect a person's behaviour. Ferri (1897), in contrast to both Lombroso and Raffaelle Garofalo, a third member of what is sometimes described as the Italian Positive School of criminology, therefore tried to broaden positivist analyses of deviance and crime to allow for the effects of broader social and physical processes affecting the individual.

More recent versions of explanations such as these are to be found in the work of Ernst Kretschmer, William Sheldon and Sheldon and Eleanor Glueck. Kretschmer (1951) claimed to have identified the existence of three body types; the asthenic (thin and delicate), the athletic (strong and muscular) and the pyknic (broad and fat) – each linked to distinctive forms of psychological illness. Pyknic individuals, for example, were more likely to experience manic-depressive disturbance (characterized by dramatic swings of mood from extreme happiness to despair) whereas asthenic and athletic individuals were more prone to schizophrenia. Sheldon (1949) also identified the existence of three similar body types: the ectomorph, the mesomorph and the endomorph, but argued that individuals differ in the extent to which they share different amounts of each of these three bodily characteristics. For him, ectomorphy (being thin, fragile and tall) was associated with being unpredictable, anxious and shy; mesomorphy (being muscular and strong) with being energetic, competitive and outward-going; and endomorphy (being round and fat) with being amiable and loving of physical comfort. Glueck and Glueck's (1956) work among delinquent boys claims to show that a

18

combination of endomorphic and mesomorphic characteristics is likely to be the best predictor of marked antisocial behaviour.

Activities

1 Make a list of ten people you know well and give each person a rank between 1 and 10 depending on how amiable or shy you think they are (1 goes to the most amiable and 10 to the person who is most shy). Then rate these same ten people in terms of how endomorphic or ectomorphic they are (1 goes to the most endomorphic and 10 to the most ectomorphic). Now look at these two sets of ratings. Do they match each other? Hold a discussion about any similarities and differences in the ratings. Discuss what these findings mean for Sheldon's theory.

Modern biological explanations of deviance

So far we have looked at a number of classical biological positivist studies of deviance. In more recent accounts of the type, where once again the emphasis lies in explaining actions which are both *deviant* and *criminal*, the emphasis shifts, however, from an analysis of the relationship between a person's body and their behaviour to an exploration of the relationship between an individual's physiological and biological makeup and their psychology. Three areas of interest, in particular, have excited social scientists. These are chromosomes, deviance and 'double males'.

Chromosomes, deviance and 'double males'

Normal male cells have one X chromosome and one Y chromosome whereas normal female cells have two X chromosomes. In rare cases, however, an X chromosome may be absent in an individual or additional chromosomes may be present. For example, just over one in a thousand male children are born with the combination XXY (Klinefelter's syndrome). As adults, these men are likely to be sterile and of below average intelligence. Similarly, about one in a thousand male children are born with the combination XYY. Other chromosomal patterns are also possible including XO in women (one X chromosome only) and more rarely XXYY, XXXYY in men.

In the mid-1960s, William Price carried out a study of the inmates of Carstairs Hospital in Scotland, a high security institution for mental patients showing dangerous forms of behaviour. Of those surveyed (342), nine were found to have the genetic makeup XYY, a combination which in the eyes of the popular press at the time made them 'double males'. When they were investigated more fully it was found that these individuals tended to be of above average height and psychopathic in nature, showing little remorse for their previous actions. Additionally, they tended to come from family backgrounds in which there was no history of previous crime. Such findings were in sharp contrast to inmates of the same hospital who were genetically XY in their constitution. Price (1966) concluded that the presence of an extra Y chromosome in men was likely to predispose them towards criminal violence.

These conclusions have subsequently been challenged on several grounds. Theodore Sarbin and Jeffrey Miller (1970), for example, have pointed out that surveys of the general population outside prisons and psychiatric institutions suggest that men with the genetic makeup XYY are no more likely than others to commit violent acts. Additionally, H. Hunter (1966) has argued that the larger physical size of men with an extra Y chromosome may in fact influence the decisions made by courts and psychiatrists, making it more likely that the individuals concerned will be committed to special hospitals on the grounds of public safety. Finally, Ian Taylor, Paul Walton, and Jock Young (1973) have argued that the physical appearance of men with XYY makeup may exclude them from 'normal' social interaction, making it more likely that they will be attracted to illegitimate activities.

Activities

1 Make a point of watching as many children's television programmes as you can for three days and note down all the 'heroes', 'heroines' and 'villains' who appear in them. Make a note also of their relative size. Hold a discussion about any relationships you find between size and villainy.
2 Carry out a similar exercise to that above looking at crime series on television.

Extroversion and deviance

Another more modern biological-positivist theory of deviance has been proposed by Hans Eysenck, a psychologist who has devoted much of his life to exploring the relationship between biology and behaviour. According to Eysenck (1970) a person's genetic constitution is likely to determine, not only the extent to which they are introvert (withdrawn) or extrovert (outward-going), but also the ease with which they learn from past experience. Introverts learn easily from their past experience whereas extroverts condition less readily. Hence, extroverts are less likely to conform to the norms of a particular society, making it more likely that they will become involved in deviant and possibly criminal acts. From his studies of prison populations (notice once again this tendency to equate deviance with criminality) Eysenck concludes that extroversion is inextricably linked to norm-breaking behaviour.

Eysenck's theory, too, has been criticized on a number of grounds since some researchers have actually found an over-representation of introverts in prison populations (Hoghughi and Forrest 1970). Others have accused his theories of *reductionism*, in that they take complex patterns of social behaviour and try to reduce these to the effects of ill-defined and obscure biological processes. For example, is it reasonable to suppose that forms of deviance as diverse as drug abuse, violent behaviour, and cheating can all be explained in terms of one fundamental biological difference – the extent to which an individual is extrovert or introvert? Finally, since it is unlikely that those in prison are representative of the population at large, some doubts must be expressed about the usefulness of this theory in explaining deviance within the general population.

Biology and male homosexual behaviour

So far, our consideration of biological-positivist explanations has looked at theories which attempt to explain behaviours which are both deviant and criminal. For our final example of this type of account, we shall look instead at explanations which have been offered for forms of behaviour which are not necessarily either criminal or deviant.

As was explained in Chapter 1, attitudes to male homosexual behaviour have varied widely across cultures and over time. In some societies, male homosexuality has been afforded high status, in others it has been denigrated and suppressed. In the light of this diversity, it seems strange that biological explanations should have much to offer. After all, is it really reasonable to suggest that the variations in patterns of male homosexual practice take place because of biological differences between men in different cultures and at different points in history? In spite of this implausibility, some researchers have attempted to construct biological explanations of male homosexual behaviour. Many of these focus on the role played by male and female sex hormones in affecting the development of the brain before birth.

Jan Raboch and Iva Sipova (1974), for example, have argued that the origins of male homosexual behaviour can be found in the balance between androgen (male sex hormone)

22

and oestrogen (female sex hormone) which affects the foetus before birth. Particular combinations of hormones from both the child and mother (the authors are very vague about what these might be) are therefore said to predispose some male children towards homosexuality and, incidentally according to this theory, higher than average IQ. Similarly, Gunter Dorner (1974) has argued that some male children will develop 'predominantly female-differentiated brains' before birth as a result of the influence of particular levels of maternal hormones.

Apart from the vagueness of such claims (the authors fail to spell out in any detail the nature of the processes they describe) such explanations fail to pass some basic tests of logic. Why, for example, would two men each with a 'predominantly female-differentiated brain' wish to have sexual relations with one another? Why should patterns of male homosexual behaviour vary historically and cross-culturally in the way they do? In common with many other biological-positivist explanations of deviance, such accounts are basically *reductionist* in their emphasis. They reduce what are complex social processes and outcomes to overly simple causes.

Social ecological theories of deviance – the work of the Chicago School

Most of the positivist explanations of deviance so far described argue that the causes of deviant behaviour are to be found within the individual. This sort of explanation is extremely powerful and many biological- and psychological-positivist explanations of deviance have actually become people's 'commonsense' ways of understanding deviance because they have been so widely popularized. However, there also exists a rather different type of positivist explanation which argues that the causes of deviant behaviour are more often to be found outside the person, in society as a whole.

23

The origins of this alternative approach to explaining deviance can be found in the writings of the French lawyer Andre-Michel Guerry and the Belgian mathematician, Lambert Quetelet. In the early 1800s, they published research which showed that while the incidence of types of deviance such as illegitimacy, suicide and violence varied widely according to geographic *region*, within a particular *locality*, levels of deviance remained relatively constant over time.

These findings suggest that the causes of deviant behaviour might best be found not within the individuals who commit deviant acts but within society itself. Similar ideas were also put forward by later writers such as Georg Simmel (1969) whose essay *The Metropolis and Mental Life* explored some of the psychological and social consequences of city living. It was not, however, until the work of a group of researchers based at the University of Chicago in the 1920s, of whom the most famous are perhaps Robert Park, Ernest Burgess and Roderick McKenzie, that theories such as these came to be explored more systematically.

In their writing, Park, Burgess and McKenzie (1925) developed what has subsequently been called a *social ecological* approach to explaining city life in general and crime and deviance in particular. Burgess, for example, argued that cities consist of a number of natural areas which develop in an orderly and predictable manner rather like the natural habitats in which plants and animals coexist, hence the use of the term 'social ecology'. On the basis of his research in Chicago, Burgess claimed that as you move out from the Central Business District of an urban area to the suburbs, you pass through a series of zones – the Zone of Transition, the Working Class Zone characterized by two- and three-family households, the Old City Neighbourhood Zone of one family houses to finally reach the Commuter Zone. The development of each of these areas, he believed, took place as a result of the (supposed) natural human tendency to compete for space. *Competition* between groups within cities therefore led to the *domination* of some groups over others. This in turn caused an orderly *succession* within neighbourhoods as predictable patterns of land use emerged.

Park extended this work to offer an explanation for the different types of behaviour to be found in urban areas. His research in the red light and vice districts of Chicago led him to identify the existence of what he called *moral regions* within the city. Some of these were environments where divergent moral codes prevailed, in which prostitution, alcoholism, drug addiction and gangsterism were accepted ways of life. In particular, the Zone of Transition was the most likely environment in which to find statistically deviant forms of behaviour, since it was the zone most likely to experience *social disorganization* as, on the one hand, the Central Business District expanded and, on the other, its own more affluent residents moved outwards to live in more salubrious residential areas.

Other researchers at the University of Chicago in the inter-war period, turned their attention to the study of adult and juvenile crime, gambling, suicide and serious mental disturbance in inner city areas, arguing that all of these could ultimately be explained in terms of the social ecology of different neighbourhoods. Among the more famous investigations of this type was Robert Faris and Warren Dunham's (1939) study of schizophrenia. Schizophrenia is normally diagnosed in individuals who experience a severe distortion of reality accompanied by hallucinations or delusions. In their work, Faris and Dunham looked at the relationship between where in the city individuals lived and the likelihood of their being admitted to public mental health institutions. They found that the highest rates of schizophrenia in Chicago were to be found in 'hobohemia', among the rooming-house and minority ethnic communities characteristic of the Zone of Transition. They therefore concluded that schizophrenia, like other forms of deviance, was the direct consequence of particular types of neighbourhood ecology, in this case the social disorganized ecology characteristic of decayed inner city areas.

25

While the work of researchers at the University of Chicago in the 1920s added a new dimension to positivist explanations of deviance by emphasizing the role that social factors could play in causing deviant behaviour, this approach has not gone without criticism. In particular, the following arguments have been put forward against it.

First, it is clearly the case that not all those who are resident in areas of social disorganization commit deviant acts. Likewise, forms of deviance such as gambling, drug abuse and prostitution, do indeed take place in the residential and commuter zones of modern cities – areas which social ecological theorists argue are, in fact, socially organized. Exceptions such as these call for some explanation, though it is fair to say that Chicago School researchers themselves were not altogether oblivious to these problems.

For example, if we think for a moment about the conclusions reached in Faris and Dunham's study of the high incidence of schizophrenia in inner city areas, it does not take long to realize that many (if not most) of those resident in the Zone of Transition of many cities do not become schizophrenic. Such an observation clearly calls for an explanation, since Faris and Dunham had argued that it was the social disorganization of this part of the city that caused schizophrenia. One possibility could be that many of those resident here are somehow 'protected' from the influence of social disorganization within the zone. Maybe this same sort of 'protection' can also act as a safeguard against becoming involved in other forms of deviant activity, such as committing acts of violence against others. This certainly was the suggestion put forward by Walter Reckless, a graduate student of Park's who, incidentally, is reputed to have defrayed the cost of his university education by working in a cafe controlled by Al Capone! He argued that adequate explanations of deviance need to take into account, not only external social processes, but also *internal factors*, such as the individual's ego strength and sense of responsibility. According to Reckless (1956), people with a strong sense of personal responsibility are to some extent insulated from pressures towards non-conformity. However, ego strength and personal responsibility are notoriously difficult things to measure and this has subsequently raised serious problems for researchers wanting to investigate Reckless's claims seriously.

But what about those living in the Residential and Commuter Zones of cities? Are we seriously to believe that they were not involved in deviant activity? Is it really true that deviance is unheard of in the more affluent suburban areas of modern towns? This certainly is what early social ecological theorists seemed to suggest. Again, there can be no definite answers to these questions, but it is possible that in the case of forms of deviance such as mental disturbance, the more affluent residents of city Residential and Commuter Zones are able to pay for private facilities and care. They therefore may not appear in the admission records of publically funded hospitals – the institutions from which Chicago School researchers such as Faris and Dunham drew much of their data. In the case of deviance such as juvenile delinquency, patterns of policing and the reactions of courts may mean that in the affluent suburbs, deviant acts are less likely to be detected and, if brought to court, more likely to be treated as instances of 'high spirits' than serious crime – thereby creating the misleading impression that deviance and living in inner city areas necessarily go together. Indeed a consideration of 'respectable', white collar forms of deviant behaviour such as theft from the place of work (more often called 'borrowing'), tax evasion, embezzlement, and the abuse of public office, seem to be missed entirely by the social-positivist analyses proposed by Chicago School researchers.

Second, and more seriously, the concept of social disorganization itself (the factor said to cause deviance) is poorly defined in Chicago School work. Frequently, it is taken to refer to neighbourhoods in which there existed a high proportion of working women and unmarried men, and in which there is a high number of persons per household. But why, logically, should we assume that the households or neighbourhoods in which working women or unmarried men live, are any less organized than others? Why also should a high number of persons per household be taken as a sign of social disorganization rather than as an indicator, perhaps, of enhanced levels of domestic support? Essentially, as Stephen Pfohl (1986) has argued, Chicago School sociologists, being disproportionately white, male and middle class, were, perhaps, unable to look beyond the boundaries of their own cultural expectations, confusing differences in social organization with social disorganization.

Even more worrying, in much of this research, similar factors are taken to be both *indicators* and *causes* of social disorganization. Hence, high rates of illegitimacy, prostitution and unemployment are said not only to indicate the city areas where social disorganization is present, but also to explain *why* it exists. Such arguments are clearly confused, since on the grounds of logic alone, something cannot both be a sign of something else and a cause of it. We do not, for example, say that spots and a raised temperature are both the signs and cause of measles. Yet a similar form of logic is used in some of the social-positivist explanations of deviance offered by members of the Chicago School.

In summary, while the work of Chicago School researchers was important in that it introduced a social dimension into the study of deviance, the analyses they developed remain somewhat deficient in a number of respects. More convincing forms of social-positivist analysis will be explored in the next chapter.

Activities

1 In order to check your understanding of key ideas in this chapter, write down what you think positivist explanations of deviance attempt to do.

2 Now make some notes on the differences between biological-
   and social-positivist explanations of deviance.
3 Finally, find some newspaper stories which report instances
   of deviance. Try to work out whether the writer favours a
   biological or a social explanation for the behaviour
   concerned. Check out your interpretation with your tutor
   or a friend.

Further reading

*You may want to follow up some of the issues raised in this
chapter. Good summaries of biological- and psychological-
positivist theories of deviance can be found in Chapter 3 of
Suchar (1978) and Chapter 1 of McCaghy (1985). A more
extended treatment of positivist explanations in general, and
of biological- and psychological-positivist explanations of
deviance in particular, can be found in Taylor, Walton, and
Young (1973). An excellent discussion of social ecological
theories of deviance can be found in Chapter 4 of Suchar
(1978).*

3

Later social-positivist theories of deviance

The positivist theories of deviance described in this chapter share some similarities with those earlier discussed in Chapter 2 since they have been developed in broadly similar ways using scientific method. What makes them different from those described on pp. 15–23 however, is their rejection of *individualistic* types of explanation, such as those favoured by biological and psychological accounts of deviant behaviour, in favour of those that are more firmly grounded in the way in which society is *socially organized*.

Durkheim and the functions of deviance

At the end of the last century, one of the first European sociologists to argue systematically against the sort of biological-positivist explanations of deviance we met in the last chapter was Emile Durkheim. Writing at a time when French society was undergoing dramatic changes as a consequence of industrialization, Durkheim argued that sociology could provide a scientific solution to the moral dilemmas confronting society. Such interests led him eventually to enquire into the normal features of a healthily functioning society.

In contrast to the prevailing views of the time, he argued that crime and deviance are not only inevitable within society (like other positivists, Durkheim was largely interested in explaining actions that are both deviant and criminal), they are also *functional* and necessary for society's well-being. According to Durkheim, human behaviour is influenced both by organic bodily needs and by the social sentiments of the 'soul'. The latter, which take their origins from within the general social morality of the time – the *collective conscience* of a particular society – are likely to be particularly strong in closely-knit traditional communities, but become less so as modernization takes place. For Durkheim, there could be no society in which individuals do not differ more or less from each other. However, the extent to which this is true, and hence the extent to which crime and deviance take place, is determined by the sophistication of society and, in particular, the complexity of the division of labour within it. In societies that have a complex division of labour – in which the roles that people play are highly specialized, and in which people may find themselves isolated from the activities of others for much of their time – it is likely that the power exerted over individuals by the collective conscience may be weakened. In these circumstances, individuality may develop in ways relatively unconstrained by common values, and people will experience *anomie* – a sort of normlessness. Under such conditions there is ample scope for deviant forms of behaviour to arise as unchecked passions and unregulated ambitions get out of control.

However, there can also be a more positive side to anomie and its consequences since, according to Durkheim, deviance actually contributes to the maintenance of order within society. It does this in several ways. First of all, deviance helps identify the moral boundaries between right and wrong in

31

society. By doing this, it alerts people to what is expected of them. Second, deviance enhances social solidarity by bringing people together against a common threat. Third, deviance has an important role to play in allowing for change within society. Societies which are locked in outdated traditions may be unable to adjust to new demands put upon them. The existence of deviant forms of behaviour can help give signals about what society might be like in the future. Finally, deviance has an important role to play in reducing societal tensions, since it allows anxieties to be projected onto those whose behaviour deviates from the norm. All in all, therefore, deviance is functional for society since its existence, by providing something for the majority to react against, enhances shared moral values, thus binding society more tightly together.

It is only fair to say, however, that Durkheim's analysis of deviance as something normal and functional for society was not widely accepted at the time. Many of his contemporaries remained committed to the types of biological-positivist explanation which have earlier been discussed, and so to seeking 'cures' and 'remedies' for crime. Others confused the suggestion that deviance was normal for society (a natural aspect of society) with the idea that deviants are normal – something which Durkheim himself never claimed.

Durkheim and suicide

If Durkheim's choice of methodology was influenced by his commitment to positivism as a way of explaining things, his choice of subject matter owes much to the work of earlier moral statisticians. For at least seventy years before the publication in 1897 of Durkheim's book *Suicide*, researchers in Germany, France and Italy had enquired into the relationship between 'moral' problems such as madness, violence and suicide, and geographical, political, economic, social and even climatic factors. In 1822, for example, Falret had first pointed out that suicide rates rise during periods of rapid social change, and in 1864 Wagner had noticed that the rates of suicide for Protestants and Catholics differed. Durkheim's choice of suicide as an area of enquiry was, therefore, not unexpected given what Gidden's (1965) describes as the tremendous interest in the 'suicide problem' in European sociology at the time. Then, as now, the reasons why individuals should take their own lives fascinated many people.

For Durkheim, the study of suicide was to be a test case of the ability of a developing sociology to explain in *social* terms what had hitherto been regarded as one of the most *individual* of acts – the taking of one's own life. In going about his work, Durkheim drew upon two pre-existing research traditions: social positivism, and what has sometimes been called the 'moral statistics' tradition of social enquiry. Durkheim's commitment to positivism as an approach to analysing society stemmed from his belief that it was possible, using techniques similar to those of the natural scientist, to identify the external causes of human behaviour. Forms of collective behaviour which exert an influence over the actions of others could, according to Durkheim, be regarded as *social facts* – variables whose influence on behaviour can be measured. Hence, in going about his work, Durkheim sought to use multi-variate analysis, a type of statistical technique popular with natural scientists, to enquire into the origins of what he believed to be an essentially social act.

Suicide rates

In order to explore the relationship between social factors and suicide, Durkheim analysed the suicide rates of different societies and for different groups within a society. *Tables 2* and *3* show some of the differences he detected.

Activities

1 Look at one of the columns in Table 2. What do you notice

33

about the suicide rates between countries? Make a list of five possible reasons for the differences you observe.

2 Now look across the rows in Table 2. What happens to the suicide rate within a country over time?

3 What does Table 3 tell us about the difference in suicide rates between Protestants and Catholics?

4 Hold a discussion about your answers to questions 1 to 3.

5 Try to obtain a copy of the *World Health Statistics Report* published annually by the World Health Organisation. Your school or college library may have a copy. Alternatively, your local reference library may be able to help. Look up some more recent statistics on suicide in this. What sorts of patterns do you find?

Table 2 *Rate of suicide per million inhabitants*

	1866–70	1871–75	1874–78
Italy	30	35	38
Belgium	66	69	78
England	67	66	69
Sweden	85	81	91
France	135	150	160
Denmark	277	258	255

Source: Durkheim (1970:50)

Table 3 *Rates of suicide per million persons of each faith*

	Protestant	Catholic
Austria (1852–59)	79.5	51.3
Prussia (1849–55)	159.9	49.6
Bavaria (1844–56)	135.4	49.1
Wurttemberg (1846–60)	113.5	77.9

From his analysis of the suicide rates of different societies and of different groups within the same society, Durkheim reached three initial conclusions:

1 The suicide rate varies between societies.
2 Within a society, the suicide rate remains reasonably constant over time.
3 Within a society the suicide rate varies for different groups of people. He described these variations in some detail.

Explanations of suicide

Durkheim explained these findings by identifying four types of social organization which he believed could cause high rates of suicide. He called these *egoistic, altruistic, fatalistic* and *anomic* social structures.

Egoistic social structures

An egoistic society is one which encourages individuals to see themselves as particularly responsible for their own actions. According to Durkheim, many Western societies, particularly those which have come under the influence of Protestant religious teachings, show such characteristics. Within them, people are encouraged, by and large, to strive to better themselves, to isolate themselves from others if needs be to do this, and to show some scepticism for collective involvement. Getting on in life, striving to be more successful than others, being prepared to sacrifice close ties for the sake of self-advancement, are therefore all qualities characterizing societies with egoistic social structures. Such social arrangements can have many sources, but Protestant religious teaching, by emphasizing the direct relationship between individuals and God, and by advocating thrift and industriousness as morally valuable qualities, has been central in encouraging their development.

According to Durkheim, protection against the effects of

35

egoistic social structures can be provided by institutions such as marriage and the family which bind people into closely-knit relationships with one another. In consequence, it should come as little surprise that the suicide rates for single and separated people exceed those for those who are married.

Altruistic social structures

Altruistic forms of social organization are in many ways the reverse of those just described. In societies where the collective conscience is so binding that there is little distinction between the individual and the group, people may readily take their lives for the sake of others. Altruistic forms of social organization have existed in many societies. Among the Samurai warriors of mediaeval Japan, suicide was a common response to personal and collective insults. More recently, Japanese pilots have taken their own lives in wartime by dive-bombing military targets, and more recently in Jonestown, Guyana in the early 1980s, hundreds of Jim Jones' followers drank cyanide together in order that they might achieve collective salvation.

Fatalistic social structures

According to Durkheim, suicide could also be induced by the forms of fatalistic social organization that characterize slave societies. In these, oppressive discipline stifles the expression of free will to such an extent that people become dominated by the belief that their own actions can do little to change the conditions under which they live. In consequence, suicide may come to be seen as the only alternative to a life of constant misery.

While Durkheim did not believe that this type of social structure was of great contemporary significance, he did claim to detect its effects in the suicides of married women who remained childless – presumably as a reaction to their perceived lack of control over their own reproductive destiny.

36

Anomic social structures

The fourth type of social organization that Durkheim identified as a cause of suicide is one which generates high levels of anomie. Rapid economic and social change, for example, can create situations in which norms regulating behaviour become diffuse and unclear. In conditions of rapid economic growth, for example, individual aspirations may become insatiable, being no longer regulated by the pervading norms of society. In these circumstances people may strive for the unattainable and, discovering that the resources available to them are indeed limited, may find themselves falling into the 'empty abyss of unfulfillment' (Pfohl 1986).

Alternatively, anomie can be created by economic decline when the rewards that people have customarily come to expect may no longer be available to them. In such a situation, people may find difficulty adjusting to changed economic and moral arrangements, clinging instead to past and now outdated values. Sometimes suicide can seem the only way out of situations like this and the economic depressions of the nineteenth and twentieth centuries bear witness to many apparently self-inflicted deaths.

With the move from traditional to modern societies, Durkheim foresaw the possibility of a dramatic increase in anomic forms of social organization, with relationships between people becoming less intimate, less regulated, more fleeting, and sporadic. *Anomic deregulation* was, for Durkheim, one of the greatest threats to the well-being of future societies.

From the preceding analysis we can see that suicide is a much more complicated phenomenon than first meets the eye. While in most cases the act itself is obviously not beneficial to the individual concerned, it may have more positive consequences for society as a whole. Altruistic suicide, for example, may actually enhance the social solidarity between individuals by affirming the bonds of loyalty that exist between them. Other forms of suicide may have useful functions to serve for society as a whole through the role they play in organizing moral sentiments and feelings about the right to take one's life. In advanced industrial societies, for example, much debate currently takes place about whether the old, the depressed and the terminally ill (to name but a few) should have the right to take their own lives. Medical and psychiatric care is often organized around trying to ensure that people do not kill themselves. Voluntary groups such as the *Samaritans* aim to provide support and counselling for those who may be contemplating suicide with the intention that they should change their minds.

It is therefore possible to see how Durkheim's research into suicide served both to illustrate his arguments about the role of deviance in general and to demonstrate the value of positivist explanations of deviant forms of behaviour.

Some problems with Durkheim's analysis of suicide

Since Durkheim's original study, the issue of suicide has continued to fascinate sociologists. Many have tried to develop Durkheim's analysis further to add more detail to our understanding of the causes of suicide. Halbwachs (1930), for example, has argued that it is not possible to be as clear cut about the types of factor likely to cause suicide as Durkheim suggested. Often religious and political attitudes, family structures, wealth and area of residence are interrelated with one another so it is not possible to disentangle the effects of any one of these factors in causing suicide above the others. Instead, Halbwachs argues for *social isolation* as the major cause of suicide – a phenomenon which can take many forms and operates with many intensities.

Others have criticized the lack of clarity in Durkheim's writing about what exactly is meant by concepts such as integration, anomie and deregulation. Certainly the way in which these concepts operate is at times not as clear as we might wish in an account which tries to use scientific method to explain an essentially social phenomenon.

But both of the above lines of argument take little exception to the general approach adopted in Durkheim's work. For this reason, they are sometimes referred to as 'internal' critiques since they share certain basic assumptions about suicide and the most appropriate ways in which it can be investigated. More radical assaults on Durkheim's approach have come from sociologists who are critical of the value of positivist analyses in general. We will look in detail at their criticisms in Chapter 4 (pp. 47–69).

Merton and the functions of deviance

Central to Durkheim's analysis of suicide is the concept of *anomie* – a state which exists when a person's unlimited aspirations exceed the opportunities available to them. Some forty years later such ideas were further developed by the American sociologist, Robert Merton, in his more detailed analysis of a wide range of deviant behaviours. In distinction to Durkheim, Merton (1938) believed that aspirations were largely social in origin; that is, they are the products of the culture in which people live. In his view, American culture was responsible for the *social construction* of a very particular set of aspirations – the 'American Dream' that everyone can make it if only they try hard enough. Such a set of beliefs, encouraging the pursuit of wealth, power and success, is still very much in evidence in both Britain and North America today. Indeed, to reject such values is, in the 1980s, to risk being labelled a 'scrounger', a 'welfare case' or a 'red'. But what happens when, by force of circumstances, individuals find themselves unable to live up to goals like these? This was the central question that underpinned much of Merton's work.

According to Merton, anomie arises in situations where people find that they can not achieve dominant cultural aspirations and goals by legitimate means. Individuals may discover, for example, that no matter how hard they work, they can not achieve the levels of material wealth to which they are encouraged to aspire. In these circumstances, deviant behaviour may result.

> 'It is only when a system of cultural values extols, virtually above all else, certain common success-goals for the population at large while the social structure rigorously restricts or completely closes access to approved routes of reaching these goals for a considerable part of the same population, that deviant behaviour ensues on a large scale.'
>
> (Merton 1957:146)

Depending on whether a person accepts or rejects a society's culturally defined goals and the legitimate means by which these might be achieved, five *modes of individual adaptation* are possible. The first of these, *conformity*, takes place when both society's goals and the means of achieving these are accepted by the individual. The second, *innovation*, a common form of deviance, occurs when societal goals are accepted but innovative routes to attaining these are followed. Working-class involvement in vice and racketeering and middle-class activity, such as the making of false expenses claims, can be cited as instances of innovation. *Ritualism*, on the other hand, involves no special commitment to society's goals but a faithful adherence to accepted means. Bureaucrats who faithfully carry out their duties but who are not interested in self-advancement, or students who attend every sociology class but with little intention of doing more than this exhibit ritualistic behaviour. The fourth mode of adaptation, *retreatism*, characterizes those who reject both the goals and means of society. The mentally disordered, vagrants, drug addicts, and others who 'drop out' of society could be said to be adopting this particular response. Finally, a fifth mode of adaptation, *rebellion*, is possible if an individual replaces both the culturally defined goals and legitimate means to achieving these with other, less conventionally acceptable, ones. The actions of many freedom fighters and political activists can be said to exhibit this type of quality.

Table 4 shows the relationship between these five modes of individual adaptation.

Table 4   *Merton's modes of individual adaptation*

	Culturally defined Goals		
	Accepted	Rejected	Replaced
Means accepted	Conformity	Ritualism	
Means rejected	Innovation	Retreatism	
Means replaced			Rebellion

Merton's analysis suggests that deviant behaviour is functional first for the individuals involved, since it enables them to adapt to the circumstances they find themselves in, and second for society as a whole, since modes of individual adaptation help maintain the boundaries between acceptable and non-acceptable forms of behaviour.

It is important to recognize, however, that Merton drew a clear distinction between functions such as these, which he called the *manifest functions* of deviance, and other more hidden or *latent functions* of deviant activity. An analysis of the latter can be found in Kingsley Davis's early study of female prostitution. In it Davis (1937) argues that prostitution serves an important latent function for society by helping maintain the stability of marriage and the family. By providing an outlet for 'the craving for variety, for perverse gratification, for mysterious and provocative surroundings, for intercourse free from entangling cares and civilized pretense', prostitution helps to bolster and strengthen the institution of marriage which might otherwise be threatened were these desires to go unfulfilled. Such claims have since been challenged by feminist writers and others who have rightly questioned whether the existence of prostitution is equally functional for women as for men (Jaget 1980).

Early subcultural theory of deviance

Many of the ideas in Merton's work were subsequently developed by sociologists trying to explain working-class gang delinquency. Albert Cohen, for example, in his study of delinquent working-class boys, emphasizes the strain experienced by these boys when their actions are evaluated according to cultural standards very different from their own. According to Cohen (1955), lower working-class boys are unlikely to be socialized into middle-class norms emphasizing the value of ambition, self-reliance, forward planning, postponing immediate gratification, being well mannered, and so on. In consequence, in situations where their actions are likely to be evaluated by others according to these standards (in school, for example), lower working-class boys are likely to experience *status frustration*, being unable to attain the approval reserved for their more middle-class counterparts. By spending a lot of time with each other, lower working-class boys successfully adjust to this situation by emphasizing in their actions the opposite of these middle-class values – aggression, thrill seeking and living for the moment. In Cohen's analysis the subculture of delinquency provides an effective mechanism by which lower working-class boys learn to cope with alien cultural values and unfamiliar ways of trying to live up to these.

Ideas broadly similar to these can be found in the work of Richard Cloward and Lloyd Ohlin whose analysis of working-class deviance also draws heavily upon Merton's claims that deviance is caused when opportunities to achieve socially valued goals are blocked. Cloward and Ohlin (1960), however, argue that Cohen over-emphasizes the impact of the negative reactions of middle-class adults on working-class juvenile behaviour. Indeed, they go so far as to suggest that many working-class young people may have little interest in middle-class lifestyles and middle-class goals, preferring instead to strive for higher status within the working-class communities of which they are a part. How they do this, however, varies widely depending upon the nature of the community concerned and the opportunities for status advancement that it provides. Hence, for some young people, organized *criminal* responses may seem reasonable. For others, the violent juvenile gang whose activities are focused around *conflict* may be a more viable alternative. Yet another response takes the form of *retreatism* into perhaps alcohol or drug abuse.

Activities

1 The research discussed above suggests that deviance and delinquency are largely working-class phenomena. Buy a copy of a national newspaper for two weeks and keep a record of the proportion of deviant acts reported as committed by working-class young people compared with middle-class young people. Make sure that you record all the acts that are deviant, not just those which break the law. Check with your tutor what proportion of the population generally is working class and what proportion middle class. Do you find any over-reporting of deviance among a particular class? Discuss your findings with your tutor and friends.

Subcultural theories of deviance and middle-class youth

Later studies of similar types of behaviour among middle-class youth have created problems for these early subcultural analyses of deviance since at first sight it is hard to explain why middle-class youth should reject goals and lifestyles associated with their own class location. Fred Shanley (1966), for example, has documented the existence of widespread deviance among sections of middle-class American youth. His informants' involvement in forgery, breaking and entering, property destruction and arson equalled, and on some occasions exceeded, that of comparable groups of working-

43

class young people. Such findings clearly can not be interpreted in terms of status frustration or a simple rejection of alien class norms. Indeed, their existence suggests the need for more sensitive and dynamic studies of youthful deviance.

Likewise Howard and Barbara Myerhoff's studies of middle class gangs in a suburb of Los Angeles raises interesting questions about the adequacy of these early sub-cultural explanations. At first sight, the young people studied by Myerhoff and Myerhoff (1964) seemed fairly well, if some-what strikingly, turned out:

> 'For most events, the girls wore tight capris, blouses or cashmere sweaters, silver fingernail and toenail polish, towering intricate coiffeurs, brush applied irridescent lipstick and heavy eye makeup. The boys, like the girls were uniformly clean, and like them preferred their pants as tight as possible; levis were rarely seen. Usually an Ivy League shirt was worn outside the pants and over this a nylon windbreaker. The overall impression fostered was one of careful, elegant casualness sustained in manner as well as appearance.'
>
> (Myerhoff and Myerhoff 1964:298)

However, among members of this group, the theft of tyres, car radios, record players, televisions and other less substantial items was relatively commonplace, as was the social use of substantial quantities of alcohol and marijuana. In addition, a significant number of those studied regularly frequented homosexual bars, coffee houses and clubs. In trying to make sense of middle-class involvement in these forms of activity, Myerhoff and Myerhoff conclude that it may be more useful to look for similarities between the behaviour of those whom they studied and that of other groups rather than assume that the former is necessarily deviant in some way.

More recent research among British middle-class youth by the present author (1987) also confirms these findings. In my participant observation study of a group of young people studying A-level subjects at college of further education, I too found widespread evidence of apparently non-conforming behaviour. Classes were poorly attended, assignments rarely completed on time (perhaps this is beginning to sound familiar), and students frequently turned up for class appearing either to be drunk or under the influence of marijuana or amphetamines.

Studies such as these call into question what exactly is meant by the term deviance. If research findings suggest that behaviours that are traditionally viewed as deviant in the statistical sense may not be so rare after all, we may have to ask questions about how it is that particular behaviours come to be defined as norm-breaking. Perhaps some behaviours are defined as deviant rather more because they *appear* to break norms rather than because they do in fact do this. These are issues which we shall take up in later chapters. For the moment, it is important to recognize that while positivist analyses of deviance such as those discussed in this chapter are significantly more sophisticated than the biologically- and psychologically-oriented accounts we met in Chapter 2 (pp. 15–29), they may still be less than adequate in accounting for how it is that certain acts become defined as deviant in the first place. Perspectives on deviance which do attempt to do this will be discussed later in this book.

Activities

1 To check that you have understood the material in this chapter, make a list of the ways in which deviance could be said to be functional for society.
2 Do these reasons apply only to the kinds of deviant behaviour which are also criminal? Or are types of deviance such as biting your nails, riding a bicycle to work and liking the taste of sour milk also functional for society? Think about these questions and hold a discussion on them.

Further reading

Chapters 6 and 7 of Pfohl (1986) provide an interesting account of functionalist explanations of deviance as do pp. 23–26 in Goode (1984). You might also find it interesting to read some of Durkheim's work on suicide. If you can obtain a copy of Suicide, have a look in it at the sections on egoistic, altruistic and anomic suicide. A reprint of Myerhoff and Myerhoff's study of middle-class deviance can be found in a collection of essays called Juvenile Delinquency edited by Giallombardo (1976).

4

Interactionist theories of deviance

The theories of deviance so far looked at have been broadly positivist in their emphasis, in that they attempt to identify clear-cut *causes* of deviant behaviour. In this chapter, we shall look at a rather different way of understanding and explaining deviance; that developed by *interactionist* sociologists.

In contrast to positivist sociologists, interactionists, or anti-positivists as some writers call them, work with relative rather than absolute definitions of deviance. That is, they argue that there are no behaviours that are intrinsically deviant. Instead, deviant actions are simply those which are *defined as deviant* within a particular culture or setting. It follows from this that there can be no individuals who are intrinsically deviant either. Rather, the behaviour that people exhibit may some-times be labelled deviant by others, but on other occasions it may be regarded as acceptable and even normal.

Interactionists, therefore, are interested in the *social processes* by which particular behaviours come to be understood as deviant and in the consequences of these for those who are labelled deviant. They are much less interested, if at all, in the cause of the behaviour that is labelled deviant.

The origins of interactionist theories of deviance

While interactionist and anti-positivist explanations of deviance came to the fore in the 1960s and 1970s, their origins can be traced back to arguments between philosophers in the eighteenth and nineteenth centuries. At that time, there existed some tension between the rationalist philosophical approaches that gave rise to positivism as way of studying the social world and the idealist philosophical analyses that encouraged the development of sociological theories that explain people's actions in terms of *meanings*. For anti-positivist and interactionist sociologists, the best explanations of social behaviour are those that explain what it means to behave in a certain way, both for the individuals concerned and for those who witness their behaviour. At the heart of the argument between positivist and interactionist sociologists, therefore, is the issue about how best to explain human social behaviour.

Activities

1 To help you check your understanding of the difference between positivist and interactionist explanations of deviance, sort the following statements into those which are positivist in their emphasis and those which are interactionist.
  - Steve decided to have his ear pierced because he thought it would look cool.
  - Cindy spiked her hair in obedience to the norms of punk subculture.
  - After a lot of thought, Nancy and Joe decided not to have kids because it would interfere with their social lives.
  - After a couple of years on the gay scene, Bill and Tommy decided to set up home together.

- Jean and Julie's involvement in shoplifting was largely the result of status frustration.
- The Japanese poet and author Mishima committed suicide largely as a result of the altruistic social structure to which he was exposed.

Check your answers with those of your tutor.

Because interactionist explanations of deviance emphasize the role that meanings play in the creation of deviant behaviour, interactionist sociologists use different research methods to positivists in their studies of deviance. In particular, they tend to be suspicious of research techniques such as structured interviews and questionnaires, which distance researchers from the people in whom they are interested. The analysis of official statistics is also unpopular with interactionists as is the study of social behaviour in contrived and artificial settings. On the other hand, more informal approaches to data collection, such as semi-structured and unstructured interviews, as well as participant observation, are favoured by researchers of this persuasion. By using these research techniques, interactionists hope to establish relationships of *sympathetic understanding* (Suchar 1978) between themselves and their informants through which to gain a greater understanding of what it means to commit actions that others label as deviant.

Key themes in interactionist theories of deviance

Goode (1984) has identified three key starting points for interactionist accounts of behaviour in general and deviance in particular.

1 People act on the basis of meanings.
2 Meanings arise from interaction with others, especially interaction with intimate others.
3 Meanings are continuously modified by interpretations, i.e. the meanings that objects, people and situations have, are not fixed.

49

The origins of these themes can be found in the work of three influential American social scientists writing at the turn of the century.

Charles Cooley and the 'looking-glass' self

One of these writers, Charles Cooley, took exception to earlier positivist claims that social facts exist outside individuals. For him, 'the imaginations which people have of one another are the solid facts of society and [to] interpret these must be the chief aim of sociology' (Cooley 1909:121). According to Cooley, people actively build up understandings of themselves by imagining how others see them. We therefore have 'looking-glass' selves built up out of the various reflections of ourselves that we see in others' behaviour towards us.

Activities

1 Try to imagine yourself in a situation where every time you say something, people ignore you. Make a list of the possible feelings you might experience if this happens continuously. What do you think will happen to your behaviour as time goes by?

2 Now try to imagine yourself in a situation where every time you speak, people listen with rapt attention. What sort of feelings might you experience when this happens? What might happen to your behaviour as time goes by?

Interactionists believe that our anticipation of how we may appear to others and of the judgements that others may make of us, is very important in influencing, not only how we see ourselves, but also how we are likely to act in particular situations.

William I. Thomas and the 'definition of the situation'

Our anticipation of how others see us, contributes, at least in part, to how situations come to be *defined*. For example, if we imagine that others find us boring, we may eventually give up speaking in public settings, thus confirming not only our own self-identities but the reactions of others towards us. On the other hand, if we anticipate that people will perceive us as interesting – the 'life and soul of the party' – we may act very differently.

Ideas like these were more extensively developed in the work of William Thomas (1923), whose intimate study of the life of a young woman who turned to prostitution as a result of having come to the conclusion that this was the only way in which she could financially provide for herself, led to the development of the interactionist principle which argues that *situations defined as real become real in their consequences*. This too suggests that the perceived judgements of others have a powerful role to play in confirming self-identities and the behaviour that can follow from these.

George Herbert Mead and the development of the self

The work of George Herbert Mead also led to the development of a number of concepts which remain central within interactionist theory today. According to Mead (1934), people interact with one another largely via symbols – images, sounds, smells, etc., which symbolize, that is stand for, other things. The word 'tree' for example, stands for a general class of plants. It is not one of them. The clothes I wear at college (jeans and a sweatshirt) symbolize my commitment to informality in teaching and learning. Hence we can use the term *symbolic interactionist* to describe a sociologist who is interested in making sense of the way in which communication through symbols takes place. As a result of his work exploring processes of symbolic interaction, Mead claimed that we develop a sense of self-understanding as a result of interaction

51

with *significant others* around us. While the term 'significant others' can be taken to include our mothers, fathers, brothers and sisters, it also describes all those with whom we have close and lasting relationships. By interacting symbolically with significant others, we learn to *role-take*, taking on board first of all, the roles of significant others towards us, but eventually the more general expectations of society at large.

Mead also argued that within any social setting, a *negotiated reality* very quickly emerges, as participants reach some consensus about the meaning of the situation and people's actions within it. For example, when you go to visit the doctor, there are certain roles that you are both likely to play. You will talk about the symptoms you have experienced and the doctor will try to work out what these mean. The doctor will ask you questions about your condition and you will do your best to answer them. A negotiated reality therefore emerges in which you and the doctor are assigned complementary (but not equal) roles within the encounter. Try re-negotiating the reality by, say, refusing to answer the doctor's questions, or by asking the doctor about his or her own health and the negotiated reality will very soon disintegrate!

More recent developments in interactionist theories of deviance

The ideas of early interactionists such as Cooley, Thomas and Mead have subsequently been developed in the work of researchers such as Herbert Blumer, Erving Goffman and Howard Becker.

Herbert Blumer and the role of 'interpretation'

Blumer (1969), for example, has highlighted the provisional and somewhat fragile nature of human encounters by re-emphasizing that the meanings of actions are not given, but require active *interpretation* by those who witness them. Such a claim fits well with relative approaches to defining deviance which argue that acts only become deviant once they have been interpreted by others as such.

Activities

1 While queuing for the bus, a passer-by comes up to the person next to you and gives them a £10 note, smiles, says nothing and walks on. What possible interpretations can you give for this series of actions? Do these actions have a fixed and predetermined meaning? Discuss your answers with others.

Erving Goffman, social identities and stigma

Similarly, Goffman's (1959, 1963) research into self-presentation has done a great deal to extend our appreciation of how social situations are negotiated. His work introduces the concept of *social identity* to describe the personal qualities that remain constant across situations. Before this, some earlier interactionist analyses might have been taken as suggesting that human behaviour is infinitely variable across situations, that humans are like social chameleons, changing the way they act to fit the circumstances they are in. For Goffman, this is not so, since well-practised behavioural routines, or *scripts*, ensure some continuity in the way people behave across different situations and before of different audiences.

Activities

1 Think of three very different social situations in which you have found yourself in the last month. Write down what these situations were. Try to identify an aspect of your behaviour which remained the same across these three situations. This is likely to be part of your *social identity*.

When I carried out the above activity, the three situations I thought of were being in a staff meeting at college, being in a bar with some friends on a Friday night and being on an inter-city train from Bath to London. It took me some time to think of an aspect of my behaviour that had been the same in each situation but after some thought I realized that in each of them, I talked only with those immediately around me and when others tried to interrupt our conversation, I looked rather sharply at them. This sort of behaviour, which is the opposite of being socially outward-going and extrovert, is probably a central part of my own social identity. In fact, the more I think about it, the more I realize that I do not really like talking with more than a few close friends at a time.

Social identities can also be consolidated by the reactions of others towards us. As a result of the negative judgements that others might make of them, some people find that 'damaged' or 'spoiled' identities are forced on them. Goffman calls this process stigmatization and *stigma* can limit the extent to which people are free thereafter to play an active role in managing the impressions that others may have of them. At present, for example, those who are open about having antibodies in their blood to human immuno-deficiency virus (one of the factors believed to be responsible for the development of AIDS) are likely to find themselves severely stigmatized by others who are ignorant about the ways in which this virus really is transmitted. (It can not be transmitted casually by touch, coughing, sneezing, etc., but only by the exchange of body fluids such as blood and semen.) In consequence, those who have antibodies for the virus may find that others attempt to impose 'spoiled' identities upon them – stigma that are hard to remove in everyday social interaction.

Howard Becker, deviant careers and labelling

Finally, Becker (1963, 1964) alerts us to the operation of two other processes of fundamental significance in interactionist analyses of deviance. The first of these, the concept of *deviant career*, implies that people pass through a series of stages in becoming deviant. First of all, they may toy with the idea of changing their life by becoming, say, a member of a minority religious group such as the Moonies. This may then be followed by efforts to find out more about the group concerned. Some of their meetings may be attended and their literature read. Finally, limited involvement in the activities of the group may take place before a final commitment emerges to this particular lifestyle. In Goffman's own work, he spells out the steps to becoming a marijuana user.

1 'You need to learn the correct techniques to *produce* the effects of marihuana use. If you do not learn how to smoke marihuana correctly, the effects will not be apparent to you.
2 You need to learn to *recognize* the effects of marihuana. Some effects such as feeling happy and at ease are not always associated with using the drug at first. You need to learn to associate these with drug use.
3 You need to learn to *enjoy* using marihuana. The sensations produced by marihuana are not always pleasant at first. They have to be learned to be enjoyable.'

Activities

1 The concept of deviant career can be used to make sense of many people's involvements in deviant activities as diverse as alcohol and marijuana use, railway modelling, stamp collecting, collecting money for the blind, scouting, knitting, parachuting and macramé. With a friend, choose an aspect of your own behaviour such as this and identify what happened at each of the following three stages of your deviant career.
   (a) The stage when the idea of getting involved first occurred to you.

(b) The stage when you became a novice in your chosen field of deviant activity.

(c) The stage when you first became committed to a life-style incorporating this deviance and when it became part of your identity.

Becker's second contribution to interactionist accounts of deviance is associated with his interest in the process by which certain acts get *labelled* as deviant. Interactionist sociologists' interest in the process of labelling has a long history. Frank Tannenbaum's (1938) study of the behaviour of boys living in inner city slums was one of the first to suggest that the actions of the authorities in trying to control behaviour such as fighting, breaking windows and missing school could, paradoxically, increase the chances of these behaviours happening again. Indeed, since arrest and punishment frequently served to confirm a boy's identity as a deviant, the chances were that in due course he would come to understand himself in that way too.

Ideas like these were also to be found in the work of Edwin Lemert who drew a critical distinction between *primary* and *secondary* deviation. Primary deviation can have many causes, some of which can be biological in origin (as in the case of congenital blindness and deafness), whereas others can be social (as in the case of many types of apparently 'delinquent' behaviour). Secondary deviation on the other hand, arises from the reactions of others towards primary deviation: 'Secondary deviation refers to a special class of socially defined responses which people make to problems created by the societal reaction to their deviance' (Lemert 1967:40). While primary deviation has only marginal consequences for a person's future behaviour, societal reaction to primary deviation can have profound implications for the crystallization of a person's identity as deviant.

Becker developed these ideas further in his studies, not only

56

of the *processes of interaction* that take place between the labeller and the person being labelled, but also of the *historical origins* of deviant labels themselves. With respect to the former, Becker (1963) claims: 'Deviance is not a simple quality present in some kinds of behaviour and absent in others. [It is a quality that lies] in the interaction between those who commit deviant acts and those who respond to them.' We have met ideas like these before in our earlier discussion of the different ways in which violent and destructive acts are likely to be viewed when committed by young people from different social backgrounds. Acts which may be viewed as delinquent by the police when committed by those who live in run-down inner city areas, may be seen as little more than 'high spirits' if they take place within the sanctity of a fee-paying school, an elite Cambridge college or the officers' mess.

Indeed, in Aaron Cicourel's investigation of the negotiation of juvenile justice, we can see how the actions of the police, probation (juvenile) officers, and courts are influenced by whether or not a person fits the image of the 'typical delinquent' – someone resident in a run-down, low income area. In Cicourel's (1976) study, whether or not an individual is likely to be treated as 'delinquent' and brought to court was found to depend very much on the extent to which he or she conforms to such stereotypical expectations.

In his research exploring the historical origins of deviant labels, Becker highlighted the role played by *moral entrepreneurs* in shaping public perceptions of deviance. In his classic analysis of the way in which the use of marijuana came to be made a criminal offence in the United States, Becker outlines the work of the Federal Bureau of Narcotics. In distinction to the conclusions recently reached by the National Commission on Marihuana and Drug Abuse (1983) that 'from what is now known about the effects of marihuana, it's use at the present level does not constitute a major threat to public health', throughout the 1930s, the Federal Bureau of Narcotics was active in spreading the message:

'BEWARE! Young and old people in all walks of life! This marihuana cigarette may be handed to YOU by the friendly stranger. It contains the killer drug marihuana in which lurks MURDER! INSANITY! DEATH – WARNING!! Dope peddlars are shrewd. They may put some of this drug in the teapot or in the cocktail or in the tobacco cigarette.'

(McCaghy 1985:298)

Inaccurate ideas like these also informed the actions of other groups such as the International Narcotic Education Association whose publicity claimed:

'Prolonged use of marihuana frequently develops a delirious rage which sometimes leads to high crimes, such as assault and murder. Hence marihuana has been called the "killer drug". The habitual use of this narcotic poison always causes a very marked mental deterioration and sometimes produces insanity.'

(Geller and Boas 1969:24)

As a result of the actions of moral entrepreneurs such as these, the sale of marijuana came to be heavily taxed in 1937, and was made a criminal offence in the 1950s. Things have changed since then, of course, and in at least ten American states today the possession of small quantities of marijuana is no longer a criminal offence.

In case you have found all these new ideas a little bewildering, the key points that have been made so far have been summarized in *Table 5*.

Interactionist studies of deviance

In the remainder of this chapter we shall look first of all at a number of studies of deviance that have tried to use many of the interactionist principles identified above. Finally, a number of recent developments associated with interactionism as a type of sociological explanation will be discussed.

Negotiation and the construction of deviant identities

White-collar deviance

One of the first studies of deviance to be influenced by interactionist ideas was Edwin Sutherland's investigation of what he somewhat misleadingly called 'white-collar crime'. Since many of the actions that he examined were technically not criminal offences at all, we are justified in looking at his findings within the context of an analysis of deviance. According to Sutherland (1939), the widespread incidence of embezzlement, fraud and misrepresentation among those working in American private industry is the result of *differential association* between potentially deviant employees and similar others. Being successful in business often involves,

Table 5 *Key ideas within interactionist analyses of deviance*

Sociologist	Concept	Meaning
Cooley	The *looking-glass self*	The self is constructed by anticipating the reactions of others towards us.
Thomas	The *definition of the situation*	Situations that are defined as real become real in their consequences.
Mead	The social origins of the self	We develop our selves by taking on the roles of significant and generalized others.
Blumer	The concept of *interpretation*	The meanings of actions and events are not given but require active interpretation.

Table 5 (cont.)

Sociologist	Concept	Meaning
Goffman	The concepts of *social identity* and	Continuities in personal behaviour across situations make up our social identities.
	stigma	The social judgements of others can create stigmatized or 'spoiled' identities which are difficult to throw off.
Lemert	The concept of *secondary deviation*	Deviance which is the result of labelling and societal reaction.
Becker	The concepts of *deviant career,*	A series of stages passed through in becoming deviant.
	labelling and	The process by which others attempt to impose an identity upon us.
	moral entrepreneurship	The actions of powerful groups who try to ensure that their understandings of particular actions become widely accepted.

'learning specific techniques of violating the law, together with definitions of the situation in which those techniques may be used'. As a result of being cut off from those who might be more honest in their dealings in the business world, many individuals thereby acquire identities and self-understandings which make it reasonable to defraud and fool others.

Male prostitution

Contrary to popular opinion, the majority of women and men who become prostitutes do not do so against their will. From extensive studies carried out in both Europe and North America, it is fairly clear that many people become prostitutes from choice. An early awareness of the fact that sex with strangers can bring good money frequently encourages young people to associate with those who are already prostitutes. A developing awareness of the high financial rewards that can be gained from prostitution often encourages a 'drift' (Matza 1964) into this form of social deviance. A number of researchers have used the concept of *deviant career* to chart the stages along the way to becoming a committed prostitute. In David Pittman's study of organized homosexual prostitution within a male brothel in a large American city, for example, the following steps were identified:

1 *The recruitment.* This is usually achieved by advertisements for 'young, well-built and good-looking men' needed to pose for photographers.
2 *The physical examination.* This involves measurement of the young man's vital statistics and eliciting information about his preferred forms of sexual activity.
3 *Socialization.* This involves learning the 'rules' and 'codes' of prostitution such as the importance of not becoming emotionally involved with clients and the expectation that all clients will be accepted.
4 *The first calls.* This involves learning to ask clients about their sexual preferences, learning to avoid 'taboo' topics of conversation, such as personal and business affairs, and learning to receive money for sexual services.
5 *Progression in the career.* This normally involves the prostitute accepting that he will not involve himself out of work in non fee-earning sexual activities.
6 *Disenchantment.* By their mid to late twenties, most homosexual prostitutes become disenchanted with the

constraints that prostitution imposes upon their own social lives.

While Pittman's (1977) work does not claim to identify a universal sequence of stages that everyone who becomes a prostitute passes through, it nevertheless illustrates very graphically how deviant careers can take place.

Male to female transsexualism

Another study which uses the interactionist concept of *deviant career* was carried out by James Driscoll among San Francisco transsexuals. Transsexuals are people who believe that their real sex does not coincide with that of the body in which they exist. They must not be confused with lesbians and gay men who are secure in their sexual and gender identities. In his research, Driscoll (1977) identifies five stages in the process to becoming a successful male to female transsexual:

1 *The effeminate childhood.* Throughout which parents frequently respond to the boy as if he were a girl.
2 *The homosexual stage.* In which much time is spent frequenting homosexual bars, clubs and bath-houses.
3 *The transvestite stage.* In which cross-dressing in public becomes an important activity.
4 *The transsexual stage.* Throughout which surgery is eagerly anticipated and eventually takes place.
5 *The feminine stage.* At which the role of 'normal housewife' or 'working girl' is assumed.

At each of these stages, the individual's self-identity as a woman is increasingly consolidated. It should be noted, however, that while Driscoll identifies this sequence of events associated with becoming transsexual, he emphasizes that there is no evidence to suggest that each stage *inevitably* leads to the next. Indeed, whether it does this or not seems to be intimately affected by the complex negotiations that take place between the person and those he encounters at each stage of the career. Because of this, some critics of interactionist analyses of deviance, have claimed that research such as this does little more than *describe* the stages of a deviant career. It offers little explanation of *why* these stages occur, or how progression from one to the next takes place.

Careers on the soccer terraces

Yet another study which uses the interactionist concept of *career* to make sense of deviant behaviour, is Peter Marsh's study of 'Aggro' at Oxford United's football ground. In distinction to more sensationalist accounts of unruly behaviour at English football matches, Marsh (1978) claims that most of what takes place is, in fact, neither violent nor mindless. Indeed, he argues that social activity in such settings is highly structured. One aspect of this order is shown by what he calls the *career structure of the terrace*. The youngest football supporters, aged nine or ten, or *Novices* as they are known, display both a sense of group membership and their enthusiasm for the game by imitating the actions of older fifteen to sixteen year-old *Rowdies*. Members of this latter group, who form the core membership of the terrace culture, and who sing and chant the loudest, may in due course become either *Aggro Leaders* (those most involved in what Marsh calls ritual displays of 'Aggro') or *Nutters*. This latter role is taken by those who are likely to 'go crazy' or 'go mad', and whose actions are likely to go well beyond the boundaries of acceptable terrace behaviour. Progression from one stage to the next creates a *deviant career* that is followed by a significant minority of soccer fans today.

Labelling and the confirmation of deviant identities

A rather different emphasis to that just described is found in interactionist studies of deviance which have focused more specifically upon the *consequences* of being labelled deviant by others.

Stuttering

In the course of his work exploring the concept of secondary deviation, Edwin Lemert turned his attention to a rather unusual form of deviant behaviour – stuttering. Prior to his research, there was a fair degree of unanimity in studies of native American life which suggested that stuttering was unknown among those who lived on the North American continent before the arrival of Europeans. Evidence for this is provided by the fact that most native American languages do not have any words to describe the act of stuttering.

Lemert's (1972) interest in this phenomenon led him to examine the life of a somewhat unusual group of native Americans who did in fact appear to recognize this sort of behaviour. In particular, among those resident on the Pacific coast of British Columbia, he found evidence of the existence of stuttering well before the arrival of Europeans. Within the communities he studied, there was evidence of a strong tradition of ceremonial speechmaking. From an early age, children are trained in the art of oratory, and those who fail to meet the exacting standards expected by their parents are likely to suffer ridicule and approbation. Lemert therefore concludes that societal anxiety about the importance of *not stuttering* during ceremonial speeches actually increases the likelihood that it will take place.

Folk devils and moral panics

Similar ideas to these can be found in Stanley Cohen's analysis of the media treatment of fights between Mods and Rockers at British seaside resorts in the late 1960s. In his work, Cohen (1973) suggests that particularly in times of social and economic crisis, the mass media plays an important role in creating 'folk devils' around which 'moral panics' can subsequently develop.

'There was Dad asleep in a deckchair and Mum making sandcastles with the children, when the 1964 boys took over the beaches of Brighton and Margate yesterday and *smeared the traditional postcard scene with blood and violence.'*

(*Daily Express*, 19 May 1964, cited in Cohen 1973:32)

By analysing the way in which the popular press described the sporadic weekend violence between rival groups of young people, Cohen is able to show how societal reaction first *isolates* groups of individuals from their contemporaries (as perhaps Mods and Rockers rather than as young people in general) and then provides them with an *identity* (as dirty, sick, violent, and inarticulate) which others can imitate. This in turn leads both to increased levels of deviance, and to the public confirmation of media created stereotypes. Processes of *deviance amplification* like these have also operated in the case of more recent British moral panics about glue sniffing, teenage alcoholism, and heroin abuse.

The disavowal of deviance

For those who believe that labels can not be challenged by those to whom they are applied, Fred Davis's study of how those who are visibly handicapped negotiate the reactions of others towards their disfigurement, makes interesting reading. In his research, Davis (1961) identifies three strategies used by visibly handicapped people such as the blind, the facially disfigured and those in wheel chairs to deny or disavow their social deviance. The first of these, *fictional acceptance*, involves negotiating a relationship with others whereby the visibly handicapped person comes to be imaginarily accepted as normal. A second strategy, in which *normalized role-taking* occurs, often takes the form of the visibly handicapped person making reference in passing to his or her regular involvement in everyday activities. Alternatively, it may involve the person who is visibly handicapped assuming the role of comic or wit. Having successfully employed both of these strategies within a relationship, the visibly handicapped person may use yet another in which attempts are made to *institutionalize the normalized relationship*. This requires normal people to suppress their awareness of ways in which the visibly handicapped person's behaviour deviates. Alternatively, the normal may be encouraged to surrender some of their own claims to normality by joining the visibly handicapped person 'in a marginal, half alienated, half tolerant, outsider's orientation to "the Philistine world of normals"'. Negotiative strategies such as these provide an important means by which the visibly handicapped can work to actively redefine the labels imposed upon them by others.

Suicide revisited

In distinction to the positivist explanations of suicide that we looked at earlier, interactionist analyses have been more interested in identifying the *social meanings* of suicide rates.

Jack Douglas's (1966) research, for example, argues that variations in suicide rates between countries, and between groups of differing religious persuasions within a country, may tell us more about the *social processes associated with reaching the decision that someone took their own life* than about the causes of suicide itself. Not only may Catholics and those of middle-class status be more likely to conceal deaths by suicide, but Coroners, in reaching decisions about the cause of a particular death, must of necessity be influenced by the assumptions they make about a person's character, emotional state, and mental health before the incident. Such imputations can hardly be value free, and an exploration of the taken-for-granted assumptions with which coroners operate could do much to aid our understanding of suicide statistics.

Such a line of enquiry has been pursued further in Maxwell Atkinson's study of coroners' decision-making strategies. In his efforts to find an answer to the question 'how do deaths become categorized as suicide?', Atkinson (1971) identifies some of the 'commonsense theories' of suicide with which coroners operate. As indicators of suicidal intent, coroners were particularly likely to look for:

1 *Suicide notes*. These were regarded as the surest sign that suicide was intended.
2 *The mode of death*. Road deaths were most unlikely to be categorized as suicide whereas hanging, drug overdoses, poisoning, and drowning were regarded as much stronger evidence of suicidal intent.
3 *The location and circumstances of the death*. Overdoses taken in the middle of deserted woods or shooting in a deserted lay-by were more likely to be categorized as suicide than cutting the wrists in front of others.
4 *Information about an individual's life history and mental condition*. If the person had a disturbed childhood or had recently been in receipt of psychiatric treatment, then it was more likely that his or her death would be classified as suicide.

Atkinson concludes that Coroners' 'commonsense theories' about suicide have a powerful role to play in influencing, not only whether or not a particular death is categorized as suicide, but also popular perceptions of suicide and the circumstances under which it takes place.

> 'Not only do coroners . . . share the prevalent definitions of suicide in a society at any one time, but they are also in a position to re-affirm these definitions publicly and even perhaps to introduce new ones. By defining certain deaths as suicide, they are in effect saying to others in society: "These kinds of deaths are suicides, these are the kinds of situations that people commit suicide in and these are the types of people who commit suicide."'
>
> (Atkinson 1971:186)

Recent critiques of interactionist analyses of deviance

The 1970s have seen a number of attacks on the interactionist perspective from sociologists who claim that its ability to explain deviance is rather less adequate than was first believed. Jack Gibbs, for example, has identified two weaknesses with the interactionist approach. First, he claims that by being 'relativistic in the extreme', interactionism offers no *causal* analysis of the factors that precipitate acts of deviance in the first place. Instead of identifying the causes of mental illness, homosexuality, adultery and rape, interactionist analyses prefer to focus instead upon societal reaction to these forms of behaviour.

Second, Gibbs (1972) claims that interactionist analyses ignore the existence of widely accepted *norms* whose infringement is indeed deviant. Somewhat tongue in cheek, he asks his readers to imagine two people in the street, one of whom is naked and the other one not. In such circumstances, do we really have to wait for societal reaction to occur before we know which of the two is deviant? Gibbs thinks not and, in support of this, asks how it is that interactionist sociologists know what to study, if they too do not accept that certain actions are quite clearly deviant.

Objections such as these have been answered at least in part by writers such as Suchar (1978) who claims that because

'Interactionists do not concern themselves with the ultimate precipitates of deviance . . . this does not mean that [they offer] an invalid perspective on deviance. Rather than deny the possibility of understanding the ultimate precipitates of deviant behaviour, most interactionists believe that it is more important to examine those *processes* that make deviation the socially meaningful reality that it is.'

(Suchar 1978:219)

Other criticisms of interactionist accounts of deviance come from those who argue that there is little evidence to support interactionists' claims about the significance of societal reaction to primary deviation. Charles Tittle (1975), for example, has argued that studies of the extent to which delinquents relapse into deviant activity after being apprehended and punished, do not support the claims of some interactionist writers that societal reaction (in this case, being labelled as deviant) is a prime cause of increased deviance. Undoubtedly further research needs to be carried out in order to explore the relative influence of different groups in labelling the behaviour of others. For example, being labelled deviant by an individual or group for whom you have respect may well have very different consequences than being similarly labelled by those whose opinions matter little to you.

More important criticisms, however, come from sociologists who have accused interactionist studies of deviance of ignoring the relationship between deviant acts and *the structure of society as a whole*. In particular, researchers such as Ian Taylor, Paul Walton, and Jock Young (1973) have argued that interactionist interest in the *small-scale* interactions that take place between individuals has led them to neglect the *wider origins* of deviant acts and of societal reaction to these. In calling for a more genuinely social theory of deviance, the work of writers such as these has done much to shift attention in recent years to what are widely known as *structural theories of deviance*. A fuller discussion of these theories and the issues they raise will be found in the next chapter.

Further reading

There is no shortage of material relating to interactionist studies of deviance. Books edited by Rubington and Weinberg (1981), Henslin (1977) and Douglas (1970) contain excellent collections of studies of deviance carried out within the interactionist perspective. A discussion of the basic principles of interactionist analysis can be found in Chapters 5 and 6 of Suchar (1978), while a sophisticated critique of this approach can be found in Chapter 5 of Taylor, Walton, and Young (1973). If you are making a detailed study of different approaches to understanding suicide, you should try to read a short paper by Maxwell Atkinson in Cohen (1971).

5

Structural theories of deviance

So far we have looked at a number of rather different ways of defining and explaining deviance. Some of these have worked with absolute definitions of deviance and have sought to explain deviant behaviour in terms of biological, psychological and social factors. Others have started from more relative definitions of deviance and have focused on how certain acts become labelled as deviant, as well as the consequences of labelling for those who are labelled. According to many contemporary sociologists, however, what all of these approaches lack are two things: first, an appreciation of the role that *power* plays in defining some actions as deviant and others as normal, and second, a sensitivity towards the *broader social context* within which deviance takes place.

The first of these concerns relates to the fact that some groups have more power than others to define certain actions as normal and others as deviant. Ideas like these, which have been eloquently expressed in Edwin Schur's analysis of what he calls the *deviantizing process*, suggest that deviance is perhaps best understood

> 'At both individual and collective levels [as] a kind of putting down [of] those who in some way or other offend. In a sense all those who have been designated deviant comprise, by virtue of such treatment, some kind of have-not class.'
>
> (Schur 1980:6–7)

The second of these concerns was touched on towards the end of the last chapter and relates to the fact that interactionist accounts of deviance, by focusing on the small-scale interactions that take place between people, under-emphasize the broader context surrounding these acts. In this chapter, we will therefore explore a number of theories of deviance which try to remain sensitive to criticisms such as these. Because they all emphasize the relationship between deviance and the structure of society as a whole, these theories are often called *structural* theories of deviance.

The nature and origins of structural theories of deviance

Structural theories of deviance start from a number of assumptions which make them different from the positivist and interactionist accounts of deviance we have looked at so far. Like interactionist accounts, however, they operate with *relative* definitions of deviance. That is, they argue that actions are not intrinsically deviant. They have to be labelled as such before they become so. Structural theories of deviance differ from interactionist ones though, in that they try to explain why it is that certain actions are more likely to become understood as deviant. By asking questions about in whose interests dominant norms and expectations exist, and in whose interests it is that those who break these norms should be labelled deviant, structuralist theories try to explain deviance in terms of the structure of society as a whole.

71

Pluralist conflict theory

Structural theories of deviance have two rather different sets of origins. The first of these, although the less influential so far as modern structural accounts of deviance are concerned, is to be found in the work of a group of American researchers who, from the late 1930s onwards, attempted to develop a *pluralist conflict theory* of deviance. One of the earliest of these writers, Thorsten Sellin, argued that as societies became more complex, and as individuals spent more of their time in the company of a plurality of specialized groups (the family group, the work group, the play group, the political groups, etc.), there was a greater likelihood of conflict:

> 'The more complex a culture becomes, the more likely it is that the number of normative groups which affect a person will be large, and the greater is the chance that the norms of these groups will fail to agree, no matter how much they may overlap as a result of a common acceptance of certain norms.'

(Sellin 1938:29)

Similar ideas were also expressed by George Vold (1958) who saw conflict as a 'principal and essential' social process. According to him, society consists of a multitude of interest groups, each of which is involved in a struggle for advantage over the others. In furthering their interests, some groups may try to gain political power or enlist the help of government and law makers. Others may involve themselves in more obvious power struggles such as strikes, direct action and political terrorism in order to achieve their goals.

The work of another researcher, Austin Turk, also points to the existence of power struggles between different groups in society over what constitutes deviance and deviant behaviour. Like many other pluralist conflict theorists, Turk (1969) believed that behaviour itself could not be intrinsically deviant. Instead, the term deviant is a status conferred upon certain types of behaviour. To understand deviance more fully, we therefore need to appreciate the struggles that take place between the *authorities* which create, interpret, and enforce right and wrong standards and the *subjects* who have deviant identities conferred upon them. Whether or not a particular set of behaviours is likely to be seen as deviant will therefore depend on how *organized* and *sophisticated* authorities and subjects are in their negotiations with one another.

While American pluralist conflict theory had an important role to play in introducing the concept of power into an analysis of deviance, it left certain questions un-answered. First, it had little to say about who the powerful are and what their relationships to one another might be. C. Wright Mills' studies of American power elites, for example, had earlier suggested that these were central questions to be asked. In these, Mills (1959) identifies the existence of 'an interlocking network of economic, political and military interests' (Pfohl 1986) influencing American life. Second, pluralist conflict theory had little to say about the *historical origins* of particular power struggles about what was deviant and what was normal behaviour, or the political interests that these struggles represent. Both of these problems are tackled more directly by recent developments within Marxist conflict theory.

Marxist conflict theory

While much of Karl Marx's own writing on deviance was restricted to an analysis of types of behaviour that were both deviant and criminal, he argues that deviance is largely the product of the way in which society as a whole is organized and how, in particular, the economy is structured. According to Marx (1965), for a society to survive, physical resources, workers, and technology must be brought together to produce the material necessities of everyday life. How this is done, however, varies substantially from society to society. In early societies, everyone who was able to worked together in order that the group as a whole could survive. In feudal societies a

73

more complex division of labour existed in which some people carried out manual labour (the peasants and serfs) while others 'organized' the production that took place (the nobles, ecclesiasts, etc.). Every economic system therefore gives rise to distinctive *social relations* between groups. These vary in terms of how equal or unequal they are.

Capitalist economies, in which production takes place for profit, also give rise to distinctive social relations between their members. In particular, a major division exists between those who *own the means of production*, and whose main interest lies in the maximization of profit, and those who *sell their labour* for wages. This relation gives rise to two broad social groupings – the *capitalist class* and the *working class*. Around this basic division, however, other less obvious ones are structured, each of which gives rise to a class of individuals who live under different material conditions.

Advanced capitalist societies such as Britain and America contain a variety of class locations intermediate between the capitalist class and the working class. Some people, while being wage earners, are required to carry out 'camouflage work' to protect capitalist class interests. Teachers, youth workers, and media personalities, for example, who encourage young people to think that profit-making is a good thing, that competitiveness, individualism and patriotism are desirable qualities in a person, and that anyone who questions any of this must either be 'subversive' or worse still, a 'communist', play an active role in helping reproduce capitalist social relations. Such individuals occupy what Erik Wright (1978) has called *contradictory class locations* within the capitalist economic system. They are, he says, neither capitalist, since they do not own the means of production, nor working class, since their actions run contrary to the interests of ordinary people who would have much to gain were capitalism to be replaced by an economic system more attuned to social justice.

Modern Marxist writers have argued that the influence of the capitalist class does not end here, however, since the owners of the means of production seek to extend their influence over not merely working conditions but all aspects of social life. In distinction to positivists, many of whom believe there is consensus in society, Marxist sociologists argue that society is divided both socially and ideologically.

Activities

1 Marxist sociologists claim that society is divided ideologically as well as socially. In saying this, they alert us to the fact that not only are there different social classes, but that these social classes may have different *interests*. To identify the existence of these competing interests, sort the following statements into pairs which express *opposing* views. Which of Marx's two broad social classes do you think would agree with each statement?

- Strikes are one of the few ways in which workers can exert an influence over their pay and conditions of employment.
- It is right that those who have a great deal of wealth should not be taxed heavily because they have earned it.
- The shareholders of major companies want their employees to be paid a fair wage for the work they do.
- Taxes on rich people should be much higher than at present because they have made their wealth largely by exploiting ordinary working people.
- All that the shareholders of companies are interested in is maximizing the return they get on their shares.
- Strikes are unnecessary and counter-productive because they interfere with the smooth running of industry for the benefit of owners, management and workers alike.

For Marxist sociologists, there can be no consensus in society, only the opposed interests of capitalist-class and working-class people. According to the modern Marxist

75

writer, Louis Althusser (1972), it is the task of state institutions such as the police and judiciary, the *repressive state apparatuses*, as well as of the educational and social welfare systems, the *ideological state apparatuses*, to ensure that capitalist production continues to take place smoothly. By and large, capitalist social relations are thereby reproduced by the actions of everyday people who uncritically accept the world as it is, as 'natural', 'normal' and 'inevitable'.

In view of the extent to which ideas such as these have influenced recent research into deviance, in the remainder of this chapter we will explore in more detail a number of Marxist studies of deviant behaviour. These all adopt a structural emphasis in that they try to relate instances of deviance to the broader economic and social structure of society as a whole.

Marxist theories of deviance

One of the first sociologists to take Marx's basic ideas seriously and apply them to the study of deviance was Willem Bonger. While much of Bonger's (1916) research also looks at actions that are both deviant *and criminal*, his work is useful in that it directs our attention to the way in which the capitalist mode of production can distort people's natural social instincts in such a way that deviance results. According to Bonger, everyone is born with a social predisposition towards altruism and helping others. Capitalism, however, makes people less sensitive to suffering around them and encourages a self-centred *egoism* at the expense of our natural desire to help others. Profit making and competition leads to lack of compassion for the misfortunes of those around us, and the desire to better oneself at all costs leads many to commit deviant and criminal acts.

More recently, Richard Quinney has attempted to identify a series of propositions which summarize (perhaps rather crudely, see *Table* 6) the main features of many modern Marxist analyses of crime and deviance. Notice once again,

Table 6 *Key components within a Marxist analysis of crime (and deviance)*

---

1 America (and by implication Britain) is first and foremost an advanced *capitalist* society.
2 Within capitalist societies, the state is organized so as to serve the interests of the capitalist class.
3 Laws (and conventions) are created by the state and the capitalist class to preserve existing social relations of inequality.
4 In order to maintain order in society, the control of crime (and deviance) is undertaken by state agencies such as the police, the judiciary, etc.
5 As a result of this, working-class people remain oppressed, particularly through legal (and normative) means.
6 Crime (and deviance) can only be eradicated with the collapse of capitalism and the creation of a socialist society.

(Adapted from Quinney 1973:94–5)

---

however, that Quinney (1973, 1977) like many other sociologists, tends to assume, at least within the contexts of this analysis, that crime and deviance are one and the same thing.

The New Criminology

Concurrent with Quinney's work in America, a group of British sociologists, Ian Taylor, Paul Walton, and Jock Young (1973), brought together insights from interactionist and Marxist analyses of deviance. Interestingly, while their book is called *The New Criminology*, its sub-title, '*For a Social Theory of Deviance*', and the contents of a later companion volume *Critical Criminology* (Taylor, Walton, and Young 1975) clearly indicate an interest in issues broader than actions that are simply criminal. In their work, Taylor, Walton, and Young argue for an analysis of deviance that is both

- *materialist*, in that it seeks to explore the material context within which deviant acts arise, and

- *historical*, in that it attempts to relate deviance and societal reaction towards it, to the historical development of capitalism as a mode of production.

While they are only able to identify, in the broadest of terms, the form that such an analysis might take, they point to seven issues that need to be addressed.

First, attention should be focused on the *immediate origins of the deviant act*. An adequate analysis of deviance will explain why some people may consciously choose to involve themselves in deviant activities while others may not. It will explain how deviance can offer for some a temporary 'solution' to the problems of living in a modern society. You will remember that we met ideas like these earlier when we looked at early subcultural theories of deviance. If you can not recall having done this, then turn back to pp. 42–45 to remind yourself of these ideas.

Second, a historical materialist analysis of deviance will pay attention to the *wider origins of the deviant act*. Deviant behaviours should therefore be examined 'against the overall social context of inequalities of power, wealth and authority in . . . developed industrial society' (Taylor, Walton, and Young 1973:270).

As an illustration of such a principle, we can take the case of 'hyperactivity' in schoolchildren, a phenomenon which has captured the imagination of many parents and teachers in recent years. 'Hyperactivity' is supposedly characterized by the tendency to be impulsive in class, restless, fidgety and lacking in attention. By the mid-1970s, about a million American schoolchildren aged between six and thirteen, of whom a significant proportion were working class and black, were being regularly prescribed mind-altering drugs such as *Ritalin* in an attempt to 'control' this behaviour. Yet, according to researchers such as Peter Conrad (1976), there is 'at this stage of medical knowledge . . . no major or reliable diagnostic method or tool for (recognizing) hyperactivity'. More than this, attempts to explore whether children labelled as hyperactive do move about more than normal children have failed to come up with any reliable differences. As David Cantwell (1977) points out, 'there is a serious question whether hyperactive children actually have a clearly greater amount of daily motor activity or a different kind of motor activity than non-hyperactive children' (Cantwell 1977:525). Why, therefore, should 'hyperactivity' have become so much of an issue in recent years? This is a difficult question to answer, but a structural analysis of the type recommended by Taylor, Walton, and Young would begin by asking what it is within schools and perhaps the broader community that is threatened by the 'impulsive', 'restless' and 'inattentive' behaviour of some children. Is it the case, as Peter Schrag and Diane Divoky (1981) have suggested, that their actions potentially threaten the orderliness of an unequal society divided along class and racial lines? Questions such as these need to be asked if we are to locate acts of deviance within the wider context of power and authority relations.

Third, an adequate analysis of deviance should also focus on the *social dynamics surrounding the deviant act*. In doing this, it will try to identify the steps by which deviant intentions become converted into deviant actions. Do some people encounter difficulties as they pass through the stages involved in particular deviant careers? Is their deviance accepted or rejected by others with whom they come into contact, and what are the consequences of this for their future actions?

Hopefully, you will remember that we have also met ideas like these earlier when we looked in detail at interactionist studies of deviance. What many of these lacked, however, was an awareness of the possibility that progression from one stage to the next in a deviant career might not be quite so straightforward a process as, at first sight, it appears. As a consequence of the reactions of others towards them, some people may cease to consolidate their deviant identities. Others may backtrack on themselves, finding it more acceptable to function at an earlier stage within a deviant career rather than at a later one. Historical-materialist analyses of deviance have to be sensitive to both of these possibilities.

Fourth, a structural analysis of deviance of this type will look at the *immediate origins of social reaction* to deviant acts. This will be influenced not only by the 'commonsense' theories of deviance that people operate with, but also by the prevailing *moral climate* and the way this would have us interpret particular acts of deviance. For example, in Britain in the late 1980s heroin use among young people and soccer hooliganism are afforded high priority as acts of deviance about which moral concern is expressed. The length of young people's hair and their choice of clothing, things that were given high priority by the media in the 1960s, are less often commented upon. We can therefore see how the moral climate shifts with time.

Activities

1 In order to explore the concept of moral climate more fully, get hold of copies of three popular national newspapers. Cut out all the stories they report under the following headings: *sex*; *violence*; *religion*; and *popular music*.
2 Under each heading, sort the stories into those which report events in a favourable light and those which are critical in some way.
3 Now make a list of the things that the critical stories object to and a list of the things that the more favourable stories emphasize. Try to identify what values underlie the objections and the approval given. This list will tell you something about positive and negative elements within the moral climate prevailing at the present time.
4 If you have the opportunity, carry out this same exercise using national newspapers from a few years ago. You should be able to find copies of these in your local reference library (but don't cut them up!). Alternatively, you may have some old newspapers at home.

Fifth, the *wider origins of deviant reaction* need also to be examined. By doing this, it should be possible to explore some of the

> 'political and economic imperatives that underpin on the one hand the "lay ideologies" and on the other the "crusades" and initiatives that emerge periodically either to control the amount and level of deviance . . . or else . . . to remove certain behaviours from the category of "illegal" behaviours.'
>
> (Taylor, Walton, and Young 1973:274)

The new criminologists claim, therefore, that capitalist interests ensure, by and large, that actions that threaten capitalism itself come to be commonly understood as irrational and deviant. Future structural accounts of deviance will need to identify more clearly the role played by *economic* and *political* forces in ensuring that acts that threaten capitalism are categorized in this way.

Sixth, historical materialist analyses of deviance will need to explore the *outcome of social reaction on the deviant's further action*. Taylor, Walton, and Young see it as by no means certain that being labelled deviant will increase the likelihood of involvement in more deviant activity. Indeed, for some, being labelled as deviant may deter them from future involvement in the activity in question. Others though may persist in their activities while rejecting the label 'deviant' as an appropriate way of describing these. For example, members of the various European peace movements, including protestors at American air bases in Britain, have worked hard in recent years to subvert the definitions of 'deviance' forced on them by right-wing governments, claiming instead to speak on behalf of broad sections of the European population. Furthermore, a continued involvement in deviant activities after being labelled deviant by others may take place not because of labelling *per se*, but because it is *meaningful* for the individuals concerned. To suggest that lesbians and gay men continue to express their homosexuality after 'coming out' simply because of the labels others attribute to them is clearly ridiculous. They do this because it 'makes sense' to them to do so. Social reaction and labelling can therefore have a variety of effects – something that is not clearly pointed to in interactionist accounts of deviance.

Finally, these six concerns need to be integrated so that new explanations of deviance address not only the *political economy* of deviant acts (their origins in economic and political processes and structures), but also the *social psychology* of becoming deviant and the *social dynamics* of societal reactions to deviance. This is clearly a tall order, and it is probably fair to say that few if any subsequent studies of deviance have been able to remain faithful to all of these concerns. Nevertheless, as we shall see, ideas like these have been taken up in the work of a number of recent writers who, like Taylor, Walton, and Young, have felt inspired by the view that, 'deviance is normal – in the sense that (people) are now consciously involved, in the prisons that are contemporary society as well as in the real prisons, in asserting their human diversity' (Taylor, Walton, and Young 1973:282). A summary of these seven points can be found in *Table 7*.

Table 7   *Key elements within a historical-materialist analysis of deviance*

---

1 An analysis of the immediate origins of the deviant act.
2 An analysis of the wider origins of the deviant act.
3 An analysis of the social dynamics surrounding the deviant act.
4 An analysis of the immediate origins of social reaction to the deviant act.
5 An analysis of the wider origins of deviant reaction.
6 An analysis of the outcomes of social reaction on the deviant's further action.
7 An integration of the above six concerns to achieve:
   (a) a *political economy* of deviance;
   (b) a *social psychology* of becoming deviant; and
   (c) an understanding of the *social dynamics* of societal reactions to deviance.

Recent structural analyses of deviance

In order to explore the usefulness of some of the preceding ideas more fully, we will look first at two studies that have examined some of the more spectacular forms of youth subculture that have arisen in Britain over the past few years. We will do this, not because there are not other aspects of deviance that can be explained in structural terms, but because British sociology of youth has in recent years been very much a testing ground for Marxist analyses of deviance.

While the studies we will examine differ from one another in terms of their focus, they share five common assumptions about the nature of British society and the significance of people's responses to this as follows:

- First, and most significantly, they argue that modern Britain is a *class divided* society. The sort of household you are born into does make a difference in so far as your life chances are concerned. People do not have equal opportunities to succeed in life, even though they may think they have.
- Second, the class into which you are born and in which you are raised has a *material* significance for you. It provides certain opportunities and denies others. It poses certain dilemmas that need to be resolved and offers various solutions.
- Third, involvement in subcultural activity (be it in a neighbourhood 'gang', be it with a few friends in the privacy of your home or be it by associating with others who share your interest in particular fashions and music) is a *meaningful* attempt to cope with the dilemmas created by class background.
- Fourth, and perhaps less easy to grasp at first sight, youth subcultures are *ideological* responses to tensions and contradictions arising from people's class location. That is, the form that youth subcultures take has both a *logic* to it as well as *practical consequences* for those involved. The actions of bikers, skinheads and punks are far from 'mad',

'mindless' and 'illogical'. Rather, they represent rational responses to being young in a class-divided society.

● Finally, structural analyses of youthful deviance take the view that deviant behaviour often contributes to the *reproduction* of relations between classes. Far from challenging the existence of classes and class relations, youth subcultures often, unwittingly perhaps, reinforce these.

Skinheads

One of the earliest studies to be informed by ideas such as these was John Clarke's study of skinheads. In this, Clarke (1975) tries to make sense of skinhead style by relating this to dilemmas confronting sections of working-class youth in the late 1960s. According to him, the fierce territoriality of skinheads, witnessed by their use of graffiti to mark out 'patches' and their hatred of 'outsiders' (be they middle-class hippies, recent immigrants or those they presumed to be gay), can only be understood within the context of the dramatic changes that were taking place at the time in many traditional working-class communities.

For many living in the East End of London and in other major cities, the 1960s were a period of turmoil, as traditional forms of employment disappeared, houses were razed to the ground in the name of inner city 'redevelopment' and communities were shattered. For young people in particular, these changes created a particular set of dilemmas to be resolved – how to cope with the 'loss of a community', how to react to the prospect of non-traditional forms of employment and how to survive the onslaught of middle-class cultural values which at the time rejected 'hard work' in favour of 'dropping out'.

For working-class boys (Clarke's analysis has nothing to say about working-class girls, a point which will be returned to in more general terms in the next chapter, pp. 97–110), one way of resolving these dilemmas lay through the adoption of a youth subcultural style which attempted 'to re-create

84

through the 'mob' the traditional working class community as a substitution for the *real* decline of the latter' (Clarke 1975:99). Hence, skinheads' territorialism was an effort to 'magically re-create' the threatened working class community, their fondness for work clothes (loose fitting denim jackets and jeans, braces and work boots) was a symbolic celebration of the continued significance of 'hard' manual work, and their blatant sexism was an attempt to reassert a masculinity supposedly threatened by the more insidious (but none the less oppressive) forms of manliness practised by middle-class men at the time.

However, by affirming the importance of these qualities, skinhead style actually reproduced their existence. This in turn has consequences for the *relations* between groups in society. For example, if skinhead style validates the expression of negative feelings towards women and black people, it will also play a role in reproducing the relationships of oppression between white working-class men and those with whom they come into contact. We can therefore say that a youth subculture such as this has an important role to play in *socially reproducing* the relations that presently exist between classes, genders, and racial groups.

Clarke's study is therefore a good illustration of a structural analysis of deviant behaviour since it emphasizes both the *material* and *historical* dimensions of youth subcultural responses. These, you will remember, are hallmarks of this particular approach to understanding deviance.

Further reading

You will find a number of other studies of youth subcultures carried out in this same way in a collection of essays edited by Hall and Jefferson (1975). In this, you will find Tony Jefferson's article on teds and Dick Hebdige's on mods particularly interesting. Make sure also that you read Angela McRobbie and Jenny Garber's essay on the absence of girls from these early structural analyses of youth subcultures. You will find it in the same book.

Punk

For a second illustration of structural analysis in action we shall look at the efforts sociologists have made to explain the origins of punk in the mid-1970s. While previous British youth subcultures had drawn their members from relatively identifiable class backgrounds – mods tended to come from upwardly mobile working-class backgrounds, hippies from middle-class backgrounds, and so on – punk was unusual from the start in that as a movement it attracted young people from across the social spectrum. Indeed, this diversity of background caused some problems in early sociological analyses of punk. Peter Marsh, for example, claimed early on that punk music was best understood as 'dole queue rock' since its lyrics expressed many of the frustrations faced by young working-class people confronted by growing youth unemployment.

> 'Most of those involved in punk music have only just "escaped" from the concrete comprehensive. Others are still waiting to do so. But, in fact, there is little to escape to. It is desperation and frustration, developing into a demand to be heard, that is reflected both in the songs themselves and in the demoniacal manner in which they are performed.'
> (Marsh 1977:114)

The logic of this analysis would seem to suggest that working-class young people's involvement in punk was best understood as an attempt to 'magically resolve' the dilemmas created by labour market changes in advanced capitalism.

Simon Frith, on the other hand, linked the origins of punk more closely to the cultural sophistication and bohemianism of life in British art schools and colleges. According to his analysis,

'Outside London, at least, the most obvious feature of punk culture has been its *lack of straight working class appeal*. In the provinces, punk scenes are staffed by the usual hip kids – art scholars again, and hippies and drop-outs. Scratch the average punk band and you find an old head band. The old hippie pub crew are the new punk pub crew – same pub, different hair styles.'

(Frith 1978:536)

According to Frith, punk was essentially middle class in origin. In particular it owed a great deal to those fractions of the middle class – the painters, designers, performers and poets – whose task it was to nurture people's aesthetic interests.

'So the notion of dole queue rock needs refining at least. For the vast majority of the young unemployed, pop music is an ever-present background to social activity, but has no particular ideological significance. And in this respect, punk is just another form of pop. It is not heard as an expression of (young people's) condition. Their problem is work. Punk's concern is with leisure. The dole queuers who do identify with punk do so because they share its concerns with play. They are, in this way, bohemians.'

(Frith 1978:536)

Such an analysis is very much at odds with that proposed by Marsh since, not only does it identify a different set of class origins for punk, but it suggests that the commitment expressed by many young people towards this subcultural style was of rather transitory significance.

To some extent, tensions between these two opposing explanations were resolved in Dick Hebdige's subsequent analysis of punk style. In contrast to both Marsh and Frith, Hebdige (1979) suggests that the 'punk aesthetic' can best be understood in terms of what it was *not*. By challenging the 'extreme foppishness, incipient elitism and morbid pretensions to art' of artists such as David Bowie, Lou Reed and Roxy

Music, punk 'claimed to speak for the neglected constituency of white lumpen youth' (Hebdige 1979:63–4). By 'symbolically plundering' the wardrobes of ted, rocker and skinhead styles (the drainpipe trousers, the leather jackets, the work boots) punk self-consciously parodied the traditional working-class concerns that had found expression in these garments. By 'launching frontal assaults on established meaning systems' rather than 'communicating elliptically and through allusion', punk sought both to distance itself from reggae and the communities to which this had historically appealed (Hebdige 1979:68). Punk thereby cohered 'elliptically through a chain of conspicuous absences' (Hebdige 1979:120).

If all this sounds a bit hard going, it is! What Hebdige is trying to say is that there may well be cultural phenomena (deviant forms of behaviour, if you like) which we can not analyse in terms of straightforward economic and class-based causes. More sophisticated structural analyses of deviance need to recognize that deviant actions may have *complex* social origins. Within a particular set of economic and social arrangements, the way people behave may be just as much determined by what they do *not* want to be like as by that which their class origins encourage them to strive for. In the next section we will explore the implications of these ideas for more recent structural analyses of deviance.

New dimensions within structural analyses of deviance

The structural analyses we have looked at so far have emphasized *capitalism* and *class* as the major factors determining deviant types of behaviour. Recently, however, these views have been criticized by sociologists who argue that structural forces to do with *gender* and *race* must also be taken into account in explaining deviance. We will therefore look at two studies which have extended structural theory in this way. They both explore some aspects of deviant behaviour in schools.

Working-class girls and the culture of femininity

The first study is one carried out by Angela McRobbie among a group of teenage working-class girls in Birmingham. In contrast to most earlier analyses of youth subcultural deviance, McRobbie's (1978) work focuses specifically on the experiences and reactions of young working-class *women*. While most of her fieldwork was carried out in a local youth club, McRobbie was able to obtain valuable information about what the girls she studied did at school. This showed that in distinction to middle-class girls in the same school, who tended to be docile, diligent and conscientious ('swots' and 'snobs' as her respondents called them), the working-class girls involved themselves in a wide variety of apparently oppositional activities. Many of these transformed the school, 'into the sphere, par excellence, for developing their social life, fancying boys, learning the latest dance, having a smoke together in the lavatory and playing up the teachers' (McRobbie 1978:104). According to McRobbie, such behaviour can only be fully understood in both class and *gender* terms. By resisting the 'official, and middle class, ideology for girls in school (neatness, diligence, appliance, passivity) and by replacing this with a more feminine, even sexual, one' (McRobbie 1978:104), working-class girls display both a 'class instinct' and an awareness of the nature of gender oppression in school. In consequence, their behaviour *affirms* the value of a culture of femininity which prizes highly 'finding a "fella"', 'attracting a "steady"' and 'getting married'. Their actions thereby reproduce existing class *and* gender relations.

McRobbie's work has had profound importance in redirecting subsequent structural analyses of deviance away from a concern only with capitalism and class as the major structures determining deviant behaviour, since it emphasizes the important role played by gender in determining the form that deviant responses take. Similar but more complex themes can be found in the next study.

Femininity, ethnicity, criticism and contempt

In the last few years there has been a resurgence of interest among sociologists in carrying out small-scale ethnographic studies of school life. High on the agenda have been studies of the effects of changing economic circumstances on what goes on in schools today, and a number of researchers have tried to identify new patterns of deviance and conformity among pupils. Mary Fuller's study of a group of fifth form girls in a London comprehensive school is one such investigation. Following a period of participant observation in the school, Fuller (1983) was able to identify some fairly distinctive patterns of behaviour among members of a group of Afro-Caribbean girls she studied. In contrast to their male contemporaries, many of these girls had experienced a strict up-bringing. Whereas their brothers had been encouraged to be out of the house in the evenings from their early teens, most of the girls in Fuller's study had been given a more limited choice between 'housework or homework'. As one of her respondents commented, 'her Mum told us that Marcia likes work, she's always got her maths book, always got some reading, some book with her . . . She does that as an excuse to get away from the housework' (Christa, cited in Fuller 1983:173).

At school, the girls in this study adopted an instrumental attitude to work, conforming minimally within class so long as this was perceived by them as likely to help them get educational qualifications. Such minimal conformity clearly verged upon deviance in many teachers' eyes, as the girls arrived late for class, completed their homework for other lessons in class time and generally ignored the things teachers said that did not have a direct bearing upon exam work. Generally, the girls perceived school as 'boring' and 'trivial'. Paradoxically however, this minimal conformity to teachers' expectations of how a 'good' pupil should behave was accompanied by maximum conformity in terms of doing the work set. Assignments were regularly completed and work was always handed in. In consequence, it is perhaps not surprising that the girls in question obtained an average of seven and a half passes at O-level or CSE.

In accounting for these findings, Fuller first of all alerts us to the critical way in which many of these girls viewed men:

> 'somehow women seem nicer than men! . . . I would say that women are more understanding, they can reason things out with you. There's only a few men can do that. Men, they lose their temper . . . Men are more stronger (sic) than women. Women are more advanced, but men are more physical.'   (Monica, cited in Fuller 1983:174)

By way of contrast with the white girls described in McRobbie's study, very few of Fuller's respondents felt that marriage would be personally fulfilling. Indeed, many viewed with anger the actions of their male contemporaries, many of whom they perceived as likely to use physical violence within the home in order to get their own way. On the other hand, older Afro-Caribbean women were viewed in a much more positive light, being seen as the mainstay of home life.

In order to make sense of these perceptions and behaviours, it is essential to recognize the influence that *gender* and *ethnicity*, as well as class, have over people's lives. For the girls in Fuller's study, doing well at school and finding good work afterwards was of crucial importance, since it related so closely to their experience of being first and foremost *black women*. Education was seen as a route by which to negotiate both relative independence from men, 'I want a proper job first and some kind of skill so that I can go back to it: don't want just relying on *him* for money, cause I've got to look after myself, there must be something I can do,' (Michelle, cited in Fuller 1983:178, my emphasis), and to achieve relative autonomy within a racially prejudiced employment market. As Fuller puts it,

> 'I would suggest that the girls' cherished hopes of greater control over their future lives and their consequent

emphasis on acquiring qualifications and a "good" job are not some sort of individualistic self-improvement. Rather, they are necessary strategies for survival where the poor employment prospects and low wages which black males can command make it essential even in intact families for women to contribute financially to the family income.'

(Fuller 1983:178)

Towards a reappraisal of deviance and deviant behaviour

I have discussed Fuller's study at some length for several reasons. The first is because it raises questions about the role of gender and ethnicity as factors that determine the sorts of deviant behaviour that some people involve themselves in. By doing this, it suggests that future structural accounts of deviance will have to explore more closely the complex interactions that take place between class, gender and ethnic influences (amongst others) in determining deviance. Second, it raises more fundamental questions about deviance itself. In many ways, and perhaps 'traditionally', it would be argued that the 'minimal conformity' and 'quiet indifference' to schooling displayed by the young Afro-Caribbean women in Fuller's study is not deviance at all. Their behaviour is not overtly spectacular, it does not dramatically stand out as abnormal in any way and it may not even be apparent to many male eyes. Yet deviance it is, both normatively (since few other pupils in the same classes displayed this type of behaviour) and structurally because, by their actions, these young women actively involved themselves in power struggles within the school about appropriate and inappropriate forms of behaviour. In doing this, however, their actions were informed as much by the fact that they were *women* and *black* as by any considerations to do with their class of origin.

Fuller's study therefore alerts us to some significant new issues which the structural study of deviance will have to take on board over the coming years. In particular, it will have to take seriously the possibility that deviance may take quite different forms, and may mean very different things, for women and men. As Susan Griffin has argued in another context,

'So little of real female experience has ever been expressed. We have no familiar images to speak of our lives and our identities, or through which to voice our feelings. There is no educated or any conventional way to describe women's real experience.'

(Griffin 1981:245)

Furthermore, black people's daily experience of racism and racial oppression may give rise to forms of deviance very different from those displayed by members of the dominant culture within British and North American society. Ideas like these, which have informed the writing of feminist and other radical sociologists over the last few years, will be explored more fully in the next and final chapter.

Activities

1 To check that you understand the difference between the structural analyses of deviance that have been explored in this chapter and earlier positivist and interactionist accounts, try to decide which of the following explanations of deviance is *positivist*, which *interactionist* and which *structural*. When you have done this, check your answers with your tutor.

(a) 'In our two-year study of the hippie community at a mid-western multiversity, we focused mainly on the process by which college hippies are recruited and socialized. We believe that by finding out *how* one becomes a hippie, we might contribute something new to the more usual discussions of *who* becomes a hippie and *why*. The term *teeny-boppers* was most frequently applied to the hippie equivalent of the pledge class. These were the incoming freshmen, in the initial stages of developing hippie associations and learning how to be hip . . . Now, many students have awaited college as an opportunity to find other students of similar interests and to begin actively seeking out the likely groups of such students. Among the most visible of these groups today are the hippies, especially the *politicals*. The politicals are involved in activities that appear to be intellectual and important. Best of all, the politicals are clearly accessible. Teeny-boppers need no formal introduction . . . But as the teeny-bopper grows older, he is likely to give up on the politicals. The teeny-bopper gradually becomes aware of the meaning of the deviant political philosophies of the political leaders and becomes uncomfortable . . . His head is full of tales of what the *skuzzies* [heads and freaks] are doing – experimenting with life without the pressure of political activity. He is fascinated by drugs. Hedonism conquers political altruism and activism. He comes to the decision that the politicals are not really so hip . . . It takes only two terms to transform a political teeny-bopper into a skuzzie teeny-bopper. Once in the student union with the skuzzies, he normally fights with his parents, drops out of school (either officially or effectively) and lives off his allowance . . . The skuzzie life usually lasts a year and a half. The skuzzie tries to find himself through drugs, drinking, sex and very little work. After that, he usually discovers that it is difficult to find himself and feed himself at the same time. Or, after finding a mate, he may decide that he no longer believes in free sex and communal living. At this point he may drop out of the skuzzie system and even get a haircut.'

(Adapted from Simmon and Trout 1967:27–32)

(b) 'Despite periodic unemployment, despite the unskilled jobs, Teds, in common with other teenagers at work during this period, were relatively affluent. Between 1945–1950, the average real wage of teenagers increased at twice the adult rate. Teds thus certainly had money to spend and, because it was practically all they had, it assumed a *crucial* importance. Much of the money went on clothes . . . the bootlace tie; the thick creped suede shoes; skin-tight, drainpipe trousers (without turn-ups); straighter less-waisted jackets; moleskin or satin collars to the jackets; and the addition of vivid colours . . . I see this choice of uniform as, initially, an attempt to buy status (since the clothes chosen were originally worn by upper-class dandies) . . . It's symbolic cultural meaning for the Teds becomes explicable as both an expression of their social reality (basically outsiders and forced to live by their wits) and their social aspirations (basically an attempt to gain high, albeit grudging, status for an ability to live smartly, hedonistically and by their wits in an urban setting).'

(Adapted from Jefferson 1975:85–86)

(c) 'Clothed in dreadlocks and "righteous ire" the Rastaman effects a spectacular resolution of the material contradictions which oppress and define the West Indian community. He deciphers "sufferation", that key term in the expressive vocabulary of ghetto culture, naming its historical causes (colonialism, economic exploitation) and promising deliverance through exodus to "Africa". He is the living refutation of Babylon (contemporary capitalist society), refusing to deny his stolen history. By a perverse and wilful transformation, he turns poverty and exile into "signs of grandeur", tokens of his own esteem, tickets which will take him home to Africa and Zion when Babylon is overthrown.'

(Hebdige 1979:34)

(d) 'At the sight of that skull, I seemed to see all of a sudden, lighted up as a vast plain under a flaming sky, the problem of the nature of the criminal – an atavistic being who reproduces in his person the ferocious instincts of primitive humanity and the inferior animals. Thus were

95

explained anatomically the enormous jaws, high cheek bones, prominent superciliary arches, solitary lines in the palms, extreme size of the orbits, handle shaped or sensile ears found in criminals, savages and apes, insensitivity to pain, extremely acute sight, tattooing, excessive idleness, love of orgies and the irresistible craving for evil for its own sake, the desire not only to extinguish life in the victim, but to mutilate the corpse, tear the flesh and drink its blood.'

(Lombroso 1911:14)

Further reading

If you are interested in reading some further sociological accounts of youth subcultures, then you'll find Brake's (1985) summary of research into youth subculture interesting. It also contains some material on recent North American youth subcultures. O'Donnell's (1985) book in this series deals with similar issues. Campbell's (1984) research among youth gangs in New York offers a particularly graphic account of young women's involvement in organized gang activities. Hebdige's (1979) analysis of youth subcultural style makes fascinating, if somewhat challenging, reading. More journalistic accounts of modern European youth subcultures can be found in books by Burchill and Parsons (1978), York (1980) and Polhemus and Proctor (1984). Knight's (1982) book called Skinheads *and Coon's (1982) book on punk are both richly illustrated and contain some interesting quasi-sociological comments. Additionally, magazines such as* The Face *and* ID *also from time to time contain some sociologically inspired analyses of young people's deviance.*

Griffin (1985) provides a good feminist account of young women's transition from school to work which makes some useful points about normality and deviance so far as women are concerned.

6

New directions in the sociology of deviance

In this book, you have been introduced to some of the major debates that have taken place about what deviance is and how best it can be explained. We began by examining some of the ways in which deviance has been defined, and a major distinction was made between absolute and relative definitions of deviance. Next, we looked at different explanations of deviance. Another important distinction was drawn between those which are *positivist* in their emphasis and those which are either *interactionist* or *structural*. These three broad types of explanation have, until very recently, formed the main substance of most sociological accounts of deviance. You will find them referred to in almost any textbook that attempts to summarize research in this field, and most sociologists who have actually carried out research into deviant behaviour would be likely to ally themselves to one of these positions.

Some problems with 'traditional' accounts of deviance

As you may have begun to detect, in recent years, things have become a little less clear cut than the theories of deviance outlined above might suggest. Systematic biases within what we might call the 'traditional' explanations of deviance have been detected since, when we look at them more closely, what purport to be general explanations of deviance turn out to be rather limited in their scope. Theories that have been regarded as explanations of all human behaviour are, in fact, often little more than discussions of *male* behaviour and male forms of deviance.

In an excellent account of this problem, Eileen Leonard points out that among sociologists mentioned earlier in this book, 'Merton made no attempt to apply his typology to women' (Leonard 1982:57), 'Albert Cohen . . . only discusses females briefly' (Leonard 1982:130), 'Cloward and Ohlin state that they will focus on males but never bother to explain why their situation differs from that of females' (Leonard 1982:131) and 'Taylor, Walton, and Young's massive criticism of criminology does not contain *one word* about women' (Leonard 1982:176).

According to Frances Heidensohn, these biases have arisen at least in part because of sociology's concern to celebrate the behaviour of young male delinquents. In discussing early subcultural studies of deviance, she points out that

'All these descriptions define the delinquent as unmistakably and exclusively male. Indeed, when girls feature in these accounts, it is to provide the appropriate counterpoint to the male theme. There is no balance or equality in these accounts, female figures are whisked on and off the stage, a small cast of extras without whom the plot cannot go forward but who have no lines to say.

(Heidensohn 1985:133)

Such systematic biases and conspicuous absences call for some explanation, and it is on the male dominance of

98

academic life that Heidensohn lays much of the blame. By drawing on some of Anne Oakley's work, Heidensohn identifies three crucial aspects to the male stranglehold over academic sociology in general and deviance theory in particular. First, there is the preponderance of men in the academic profession, particularly at the top. Then there is the 'founding *fathers*' emphasis within the discipline which attempts to define 'good' sociology as that which uses the insights of 'grand old men' such as Marx, Weber and Durkheim. Finally, there is a more pervasive 'ideology of gender' which makes it seem natural for many sociologists to look at men's behaviour and to ignore the actions of women.

Patriarchy and the social construction of deviance

To some extent it is possible that 'traditional' accounts of deviance have been biased in this way because, at least with respect to actions that are both deviant *and criminal*, until very recently, recorded crime rates for girls and women have been lower than those for boys and men. In consequence,

> 'Female *crime* has had therefore a low public profile, it has not seemed to be an acute social problem, needing solution, for which research funds might be forthcoming and upon which careers might be built. From the researcher's point of view these features have also meant that girl subjects have been more elusive, more thinly scattered; girls are located elsewhere than on the street corners or in the gangs.'

> (Heidensohn 1985:142)

However, there is another more sinister dimension to this problem as Carol Smart (1976) has pointed out. Women's exclusion from studies of those who perpetrate deviant and criminal acts is mirrored by their exclusion from studies of those who are *victims* of these same actions. Thus, until recently, the study of rape, violence against women, and sexual harrassment has been of marginal interest to many sociologists. Fortunately, things are beginning to change, and in the last few years a number of important studies in these fields have been published. Many of these ask significant questions about the effects of male power, or *patriarchy*, on women's lives. In particular, they raise questions about how this is able to conceal and even normalize men's aggression and violence towards women. In consequence, actions that might otherwise be regarded as deviant and morally reprehensible, come to be viewed as 'normal' and a natural part of the taken for granted reality of many women's lives.

Another related issue raised by feminist writers in the last few years concerns the origins and effects of *patriarchal ideologies*: sets of apparently logical ideas that have real consequences for the way women and men behave. (Perhaps you remember meeting the concept of ideology earlier on when we were talking about ideologies associated with particular class locations. If not, turn back to p. 75 to check up on this.)

Of particular interest to some writers have been those ideologies that make marriage and childbearing seem an inevitable option for many women when, paradoxically, these are the very environments that are most likely to result in serious damage to their physical and mental health. As Dobash and Dobash (1979) put it,

> 'For a woman to be brutally or systematically assaulted she must usually enter our most sacred institution, the family. It is within marriage that a woman is most likely to be slapped and shoved about, severely assaulted, killed or raped ... It cannot be too highly stressed that it is marriage and the taking on of the status of wife that make a woman the "appropriate victim" of violence aimed at "putting her in her place".'
>
> (Dobash and Dobash 1979:79, 93)

Not to be married by a certain age carries with it for many women the stigma of 'unnaturalness'. Not having children, as Elaine Campbell's (1985) recent study of voluntarily childless marriages shows, is to run the risk of being perceived as 'selfish', 'odd', 'weird' and 'unfeminine'. Her respondents found themselves constantly involved in power struggles with friends and relatives over the choices they had made. Yet, as Heidensohn (1985) has remarked,

'Marriage, domesticity (and childbearing) provide powerful controlling mechanisms to ensure the good behaviour of adult women. They are all the more powerful since they can be largely imposed with the willing, even eager, acquiescence of women themselves.'

(Heidensohn 1985:180)

Patriarchal control over women and men's perceptions of institutions such as marriage thereby structures not only our expectations and experiences, but has an important role to play in defining the boundaries between deviant and non-deviant forms of behaviour.

Control over women's lives is also achieved by men's efforts to define women by their 'reputations'. In Sue Lees' (1983) study of 'How Boys Slag Off Girls', for example, she points out how few strategies girls have by which to fight back when boys call them a 'slag' a 'bitch' or a 'slut'. Comparable words simply do not exist to describe boys. Boys' use of terms such as these therefore has a controlling effect over young women's behaviour while at the same time it sets, in male terms, the parameters of female deviance.

Finally, in the street, at their place of work as well as socially, women endure sexual harrassment by men. The form this can take ranges from 'whistles and catcalls and the fixing of pinups and soft porn pictures, to physical approaches and attacks which could be defined as possibly indecent' (Heidensohn 1985:190). In addition to policing women's behaviour, such actions also have a role to play in determining what it is normal for men and women to be like.

In the light of these illustrations it would seem beyond doubt that male as well as class-based power has an important role to play in influencing our understandings of

101

normality and deviance. Future accounts of deviant behaviour will have to take seriously the claims of feminist sociologists who have found many of the more 'traditional' explanations severely limited in their scope.

Further reading

You may wish to follow up some of the ideas raised above in the books by the following authors. A good account of women's sexual harrassment by men can be found in a book by Hadjifotiou (1983). Dobash and Dobash (1979) and Wilson (1983) provide comprehensive accounts of men's violence against women, particularly within the domestic context. Brownmiller (1975) and Toner (1982) provide some of the most accessible sociological analyses of rape.

Racism and the social construction of deviance

Another dimension that needs to be taken into account in future studies of deviance is the power of racist ideologies to influence our perceptions of what is normal and what is deviant. In a recent essay, Errol Lawrence draws attention to the role played by *commonsense racist ideologies* in structuring how many white people come to see and understand black culture. Historically, black family structures and the behaviour of black people (particularly young black people) have been judged in white terms. In consequence, the culture and behaviour of black people is frequently seen (by whites) as 'irrational', 'sick' and 'deviant'. Lawrence (1982) calls this process the *pathologization of black culture*.

As examples of it in action, he cites media portrayals of arranged marriages within parts of Britain's Asian community as indicative of 'the inherent "barbarity" of Asian cultures' (Lawrence 1982:75). Similarly, differences in average family size within minority ethnic communities are frequently interpreted by whites, not as the legacy of cultural and economic oppression (slavery, for example barbarically re-organized African family structures for the benefit of white interests), but as 'the "natural" consequence of the Afro-Caribbean's sexuality and the power that Asian men wield over Asian women' (Lawrence 1982:75).

Racism therefore may play a significant role in structuring not only popular but sociological understandings of normal and deviant behaviour. Future research will have to remain sensitive to this and will have to explore more fully the role played by racism in influencing the way we see the behaviour of dominant and minority ethnic groups.

Further reading

In order to follow up these ideas, get hold of a copy of a collection of papers produced at the Centre for Contemporary Cultural Studies (1982) at Birmingham University. Chapters 2 and 3 of this book by Errol Lawrence are well written and explore in some detail the pathologization of black culture.

Towards a unified theory of deviance

'It's all very well criticizing, but what would you put in its place?' is a comment often directed at sociologists by those working in less critical fields of enquiry. But nowhere does such a comment seem more appropriate than following a resounding critique of existing theory. If feminist writers are correct in their identification of serious flaws in 'traditional' explanations of deviance, where do we go from here? Obviously there can be no quick and easy answer to a question such as this, but in the last few pages of this book, I would like to identify at least one possibility.

One answer to this question might be to try and develop a number of *local* theories of deviance – ones which do little more than attempt to explain the nature and origins of specific acts of deviance. Thus, sociologists might seek to enquire more thoroughly into the nature of specific types of deviance within the household, in school, at work and so on. They might further narrow their vision to concentrate specifically upon those forms of deviance that most concern women, or men, or the elderly, or members of minority ethnic communities. Such an approach has much to recommend it since it would enable sociologists to focus on clearly identifiable issues.

On the other hand, there may be value in examining what it is that apparently different acts of deviance share in common. This more *global* approach would not necessarily ignore an analysis of specific acts of deviance, but might focus also on similarities between these. By doing this, it might seek to explore three things that Taylor, Walton, and Young earlier (see pp. 77–82) argued were central within an adequate theory of deviance:

1 The *structural determinants* of deviance.
2 The *processes of societal reaction* towards deviance.
3 The *social psychology* of involvement in deviance.

Whether a unified theory of deviance such as this is possible given our present state of knowledge, is an issue much debated by sociologists today, but on the assumption that it is, I will try to spell out some of the features that it might have.

Patriarchy, class and the origins of deviance

Structural determinants

In Chapter 5 we were introduced via recent Marxist theory to the important role played by *economic* structures in determining both deviance and societal reaction towards its occurrence. Towards the end of the last chapter and earlier in this, we saw that such a view has to be modified to allow for the parallel influence of *patriarchal* and *racial* structures influencing women's and men's lives. While some sociologists have seen the origins of these various structures as separate, others have argued that they may in fact be interrelated. For the sake of suggesting where the beginnings of an integrated theory of deviance, may lie, I will take the latter view, and will focus here on exploring the possible relationships between patriarchal and economic determinants of deviance.

In recent years, sociologists such as Veronica Beechey have found it useful to consider the implications of capitalist processes of production for the division of labour between women and men. Before capitalism, the production and consumption of goods took place largely within the household, but with the development of modern industry, production took place more and more in factories. Households came therefore to be centres for the *reproduction* of the work-force, both biologically and socially. In terms of *biological reproduction*, households within capitalism become, by and large, centres of procreation. With respect to *social reproduction*, they take on the major responsibility for reproducing attitudes and behaviours that do not threaten the continued existence of capitalism itself. According to Beechey (1978:194), 'The specific role of the family . . . involves . . . the reproduction of patriarchal ideology.'

For women, this is likely to result in their socialization into familial and domestic ideologies that stress their 'natural' role as 'mothers', 'nurturers', and 'carers'. As a result of this, many women come to undertake vast amounts of unpaid domestic labour within the home – work which, if it had to be paid for, would seriously threaten the profits made by industrialists. For men, on the other hand, these same processes result in socialization into forms of behaviour that control the actions of women and children under the guise of 'providing' and 'protecting'. For both sexes *compulsory heterosexuality* becomes the norm, since behaviours that threaten the biological reproduction of the labour force or weaken the link between sexual pleasure and procreation are likely to threaten capitalism itself: the former by interrupting the supply of future workers, the latter by calling into question the importance of monogamous relationships in which one partner carries out unpaid domestic labour for the other.

Processes of societal reaction

In Chapter 4 you were introduced to debates within interactionist accounts of deviance about the significance (or otherwise) of societal reaction for the future occurrence of deviant behaviour. At that time, however, little was said about the origins of moral panics. Indeed, interactionist theories in general are weak when it comes to identifying the ultimate origins of deviance. In the light of this, a unitary theory of deviance would therefore need to account for the origins of societal reaction in terms of the structure of society as a whole. In doing so, it would emphasize that concurrent with the social construction of dominant patterns of behaviour, is the production of ideologies which *legitimate* and *naturalize* these.

Ideologies of masculinity and femininity which emphasize the differences between women and men at the expense of anything they share in common, are often put into circulation in capitalist societies. Once there, of course, they have practical consequences for the ways in which women and men subsequently organize their lives. They also have consequences for processes of societal reaction to deviance as people's everyday behaviour becomes judged according to the extent to which it matches, or differs from, dominant ideologies.

People whose actions and behaviour differs from these requirements come to be labelled as abnormal and deviant in some way. You have only to look at the way in which women protesting against the presence of American military bases in Britain at Greenham Common and Molesworth have been portrayed by some sections of the British media (as 'uncaring mothers', 'lesbians', and 'communist sympathizers') to understand how powerful *dominant* ideologies of femininity and masculinity really are in structuring our behaviour and how we see the world. Were we to extend our analysis of this particular problem to look at the role of military expenditure in maintaining the continued profitability of capitalist processes of production (and the threats posed to this by peace movements internationally), it might be possible to identify some of the connections between dominant ideologies of *gender*, their use in denigrating the actions of everyday women involved in peaceful protest and broader *economic* determinants.

In time, and with careful sociological analysis, it may therefore be possible to develop a more sophisticated appreciation of how and why it is that actions that threaten the continued existence of existing capitalist economic and social relations so often become identified as deviant.

Activities

1 In order to explore ideologies of masculinity and femininity more fully, get hold of a couple of copies of magazines directed specifically at boys in their early teens. Look through them carefully and as you do so, add to the following list of things that boys like.

Boys like: football, soldiers and battles, getting dirty.

Now carry out a similar exercise with equivalent girls' magazines.
Girls like:

If you have time, repeat the exercise using magazines directed towards women and men in their thirties and forties.

2 When you have done this, hold a debate about the power that ideologies such as these have over people's lives.

The social psychology of involvement in deviant practices

One thing that may have emerged from your debate is some argument about the power of ideologies such as these to influence people's behaviour. You may also have talked about the existence of ideologies of masculinity and femininity other than those you encountered in this particular selection of magazines. Indeed, a glance through some alternative magazines with, perhaps, a feminist or gay interest could have led you to reach a quite different set of conclusions. Some people quite rightly feel that they can, and have, *resisted* the power of dominant ideologies to structure their lives, and this resistance is something that we discussed earlier in Chapter 5 (pp. 87–92). Indeed, within society there is always competition between ideologies, whether about gender, class or anything else. Usually, however, some ideologies win out over others and it is these *hegemonic* ideologies that are most powerful in structuring our commonsense understandings of normality and deviance.

An adequate understanding of why people involve themselves in what are popularly seen as deviant activities must therefore take account not only of the personal benefits to be gained from involvement in deviance, but also the collective benefits that can accrue from attempts to challenge existing relations of inequality. By banding together and asserting a collective identity that *affirms* types of behaviour that might otherwise be labelled deviance, groups such as supporters of animal rights, disability rights, members of minority ethnic groups, and lesbians and gay men, have created a countervailing force against interests that seek to preserve existing patterns of inequality. The *creative* and *liberating* aspect of deviance should not be ignored by future research.

Future accounts of deviance should therefore remain sensitive to the possibility that some groups may actively choose deviance paths in order to *resist* daily oppression within a class, race, and gender divided society. Overall, at a minimum, they will have to explain the relationship between *social structures*, the *collective meanings* that underpin deviant behaviour, the manner in which these are modified by *processes of societal reaction* and the consequences of all of these processes for *identity formation*. Achieving all of this is a tall order, but it would seem a goal worth striving for if the sociology of deviance is to establish itself on a less fragmented basis in the future.

Concluding comments

It would have been nice to have been able to end this book by presenting a coherent and fully worked out account of deviance. Unfortunately, as is often the case in sociology, the more we research into a problem, the less clear cut things become. Such has been the case here, and although we have travelled a long way our exploration of different sociological explanations of deviance, it is not possible to say with any certainty what future developments within this field will bring. However, I will end with a personal note, one that I make in response to the many people I have taught over the past few years who have, in all fairness, asked me, 'Where do *you* stand in all of this?' From my own point of view, I find most satisfying those explanations that take seriously

- the *historical* origins of deviant phenomena;
- the *material consequences* of involvement in deviant activity;
- the role of *economic and patriarchal power* in determining deviance and in structuring people's perceptions of 'normal' and 'deviant' behaviour;
- the possibility that deviance may in many circumstances be a *positive* and *creative* quality;
- the possibility that in a more equal, more tolerant and more open society than that in which we live today, there would be *no need for people or actions to be labelled as deviant*.

As a gay man I, like many others, spend much of my time struggling against the ignorance and prejudice that is so widespread among ordinary people even today, against that curious mixture of sympathy and hatred displayed by politicians, religious leaders and others who would have us believe that heterosexuality, marriage and the family are the *only* normal ways of behaving. But I take comfort from the possibility that with continued resistance, one day people may be more generous in their understanding of, and less punitive in their reactions towards, *social difference*.

References

Aggleton, P.J. (1987) *Rebels Without a Cause?* Basingstoke: Falmer Press.

Althusser, L. (1972) Ideology and Ideological State Apparatuses. In L. Althusser, *Lenin and Philosophy and Other Essays*. London: Verso.

Atkinson, M. (1971) Societal Reactions to Suicide: the Role of Coroners' Definitions. In S. Cohen (ed.) *Images of Deviance*. Harmondsworth: Penguin Books.

Becker, H. (1963) *Outsiders: Studies in the Sociology of Deviance*. New York: Free Press.

Becker, H. (1964) *The Other Side: Perspectives on Deviance*. New York, Free Press.

Beechey, V. (1978) Women and Production. In A. Kuhn and A. Wolpe (eds) *Feminism and Materialism*. London: Routledge & Kegan Paul.

Blumer, H. (1969) Society as Symbolic Interaction. In E. Rose (ed.) *Symbolic Interactionism*. Englewood Cliffs: Prentice Hall.

Bonger, W. (1916) *Criminality and Economic Conditions*. Boston: Little Brown.

Brake, M. (1985) *Comparative Youth Culture*. London: Routledge & Kegan Paul.

111

Brownmiller, S. (1975) *Against Our Will*. Harmondsworth: Penguin Books.

Bullough, V. (1976) *Sexual Variance in Society and History*. Chicago: University of Chicago Press.

Burchill, J. and Parsons, T. (1978) *The Boy Looked at Johnny*. London: Pluto Press.

Campbell, A. (1984) *The Girls in the Gang*. Oxford: Blackwell.

Campbell, E. (1985) *The Childless Marriage*. London: Tavistock.

Cantwell, D. (1977) Hyperkinetic Syndrome. In M. Rutter and L. Hersov (eds) *Child Psychiatry*. London: Blackwell.

Centre for Contemporary Cultural Studies (1982) *The Empire Strikes Back*. London: Hutchinson.

Cicourel, A. (1976) *The Social Organisation of Juvenile Justice*. London: Heinemann.

Clarke, J. (1975) The Skinheads and the Magical Recovery of Community. In S. Hall and T. Jefferson (eds) *Resistance through Rituals*. London: Hutchinson.

Cloward, R. and Ohlin, L. (1960) *Delinquency and Opportunity*. New York: Free Press.

Cohen, A. (1955) *Delinquent Boys: The Culture of the Gang*. New York: Free Press.

Cohen, S. (1971) *Images of Deviance*. Harmondsworth: Penguin Books.

Cohen, S. (1973) *Folk Devils and Moral Panics*. London: Paladin.

Conrad, P. (1976) *Identifying Hyperactive Children*. Lexington: Lexington Books.

Cooley, C. (1909) *Human Nature and the Social Order*. Glencoe: Free Press.

Coon, C. (1982) *1988: The New Wave, Punk Rock Explosion*. London: Omnibus Books.

Davis, F. (1961) Deviance Disavowal: The Management of Strained Interaction by the Visibly Handicapped. *Social Problems* 9: 120–32.

Davis, K. (1937) The Sociology of Prostitution. *American Sociological Review* 2: 744–55.

Dobash, R. and Dobash, R. (1979) *Violence Against Wives*. London: Open Books.

Dorner, G. (1974) A Neuroendocrine Disposition for Homosexuality in Men. *Archives of Sexual Behaviour* 4: 1–8.

Douglas, J. (1966) *The Social Meanings of Suicide*. Princeton: Princeton University Press.

Douglas, J. (ed.) (1970) *Observations of Deviance*. New York: Random House.

Douglas, J. (1984) *The Sociology of Deviance*. New York: Allyn.

Driscoll, J. (1977) Transsexuals. In J. Henslin (ed.) *Deviant Lifestyles*. New Jersey: Transaction Books.

Durkheim, E. (1970) *Suicide*. London: Routledge & Kegan Paul.

Eysenck, H. (1970) *Crime and Personality*. London: Paladin.

Faris, R. and Dunham, W. (1939) *Mental Disorders in Urban Areas*. Chicago: University of Chicago Press.

Ferri, E. (1897) *Criminal Sociology*. New York: D. Appleton.

Freeman, D. (1984) *Margaret Mead and Samoa*. Harmondsworth: Penguin Books.

Frith, S. (1978) The Punk Bohemians. *New Society* 9 March.

Fuller, M. (1983) Qualified Criticism, Critical Qualifications. In L. Barton and S. Walker (eds) *Race, Class and Education*. London: Croom Helm.

Gallup Poll (1985) Survey of Vegetarianism in Britain for Real Eat Company.

Geller, A. and Boas, M. (1969) *The Drug Beat*. New York: McGraw-Hill.

Giallombardo, R. (1976) *Juvenile Delinquency*. New York: Wiley.

Gibbs, J. (1972) Issues in Defining Deviant Behaviour. In J. Douglas (ed.) *Theoretical Perspectives on Deviance*. New York: Basic Books.

Giddens, A. (1965) *The Sociology of Suicide*. London: Macmillan.

Glueck, S. and Glueck, E. (1956) *Physique and Delinquency*. New York: Harper & Bros.

Goffman, E. (1959) *The Presentation of the Self in Everyday Life*. New York: Doubleday.

Goffman, E. (1963) *Stigma: Notes on the Management of Spoiled Identity*. New York: Doubleday.

Goode, E. (1984) *Deviant Behaviour*. Englewood Cliffs: Prentice Hall.

Griffin, C. (1985) *Typical Girls?* London: Routledge & Kegan Paul.

Griffin, S. (1981) *Pornography and Silence*. London: The Women's Press.

113

Hadjifotiou, N. (1983) *Women and Harrassment at Work*. London: Pluto Press.

Halbwachs, M. (1930) *Les Causes de Suicide*. Paris: Alcan.

Hall, S. and Jefferson, T. (1975) *Resistance through Rituals*. London: Hutchinson.

Hebdige, D. (1979) *Subculture: the Meaning of Style*. London: Methuen.

Heidensohn, F. (1985) *Women and Crime*. London: Macmillan.

Henslin, J. (1977) *Deviant Lifestyles*. New Jersey: Transaction Books.

Hoghughi, M. and Forrest, A. (1970) Eysenck's Theory of Criminality. *British Journal of Criminology* 10: 240–54.

Hunter, H. (1966) YY Chromosomes and Klinefelter's Syndrome. *The Lancet* 30 April.

Jaget, C. (1980) *Prostitutes – Our Life*. Bristol: Falling Wall Press.

Jefferson, T. (1975) Cultural Responses of the Teds. In S. Hall and T. Jefferson (eds) *Resistance through Rituals*. London: Hutchinson.

Kaberry, P. (1952) *Women of the Grasslands*. London: HMSO.

Knight, N. (1982) *Skinhead*. London: Omnibus Press.

Kretschmer, E. (1951) *Physique and Character*. New York: Humanities Press.

Lawrence, E. (1982) Just Plain Common Sense: the 'Roots' of Racism. In Centre for Contemporary Cultural Studies, *The Empire Strikes Back*. London: Hutchinson.

Lees, S. (1983) How Boys Slag Off Girls. *New Society* 13 October.

Lemert, E. (1967) *Human Deviance, Social Problems and Social Control*. New York: Prentice Hall.

Lemert, E. (1972) *Human Deviance, Social Problems and Social Control*. 2nd edn. Englewood Cliffs: Prentice Hall.

Leonard, E. (1982) *Women, Crime and Society*. New York: Longmans.

Lombroso, C. (1911) *Crime, Its Causes and Remedies*. Boston: Little Brown.

Marsh, P. (1977) Dole Queue Rock. *New Society* 20 January.

Marsh, P. (1978) Life and Careers on the Soccer Terraces. In R. Ingram, S. Hall, J. Clarke, P. Marsh, and P. Donovan (eds) *Football Hooliganism: The Wider Context*. London: Interaction Inprint.

Marx, K. (1965) *The German Ideology*. London: Lawrence & Wishart.

Matza, D. (1964) *Delinquency and Drift*. New York: Wiley.

McCaghy, C. (1985) *Deviant Behaviour*. New York: Macmillan.

McRobbie, A. (1978) Working Class Girls and the Culture of Femininity. In Centre for Contemporary Cultural Studies, *Women Take Issue*. London: Hutchinson.

Mead, G. (1934) Mind, Self and Society. In C. Morris (ed.) *Mind, Self and Society*. Chicago: University of Chicago Press.

Mead, M. (1976) *Male and Female*. Harmondsworth: Penguin Books.

Merton, R. (1938) Social Structure and Anomie. *American Sociological Review* 3: 672–82.

Merton, R. (1957) *Social Theory and Social Structure*. New York: Free Press.

Mills, C. Wright (1959) *The Power Elite*. New York: Oxford University Press.

Myerhoff, H. and Myerhoff, B. (1964) Field Observations of Middle Class 'Gangs'. In R. Giallombardo (ed.) *Juvenile Delinquency*. New York: Wiley.

National Commission on Marihuana and Drug Abuse (1983) *Drug Use in America: Problem in Perspective*. Washington, DC: Government Printing Office.

O'Donnell, M. (1985) *Age and Generation*. London: Tavistock.

Park, R., Burgess, E.W., and McKenzie, R.D. (1925) *The City*. Chicago: University of Chicago Press.

Pfohl, S. (1986) *Images of Deviance and Social Control*. New York: McGraw-Hill.

Pittman, D. (1977) The Male House of Prostitution. In J. Henslin (ed.) *Deviant Lifestyles*. New Jersey: Transaction Books.

Polhemus, T. and Proctor, L. (1984) *Pop Styles*. London: Vermilion.

Price, W. (1966) Criminal Patients with XYY Sex Chromosome Complement. *The Lancet* 12 March.

Quinney, R. (1973) *Critique of Legal Order*. Boston: Little Brown.

Quinney, R. (1977) *Class, State and Crime*. New York: McKay.

Raboch, J. and Sipova, I. (1974) Intelligence in Homosexuals, Transsexuals and Hypogonadotropic Eunuchoids. *Journal of Sex Research* 10: 156–61.

Reckless, W. (1956) Self Concept as an Insulator Against Delinquency. *American Sociological Review* 21: 744–56.

Rubington, E. and Weinberg, M. (1981) *Deviance: The Interactionist Perspective*. New York: Macmillan.

Sarbin, T. and Miller, J. (1970) Demonism Re-Visited: The XYY Chromosomal Anomality. *Issues in Criminology* 5: 195–207.

Schrag, P. and Divoky, D. (1981) *The Myth of the Hyperactive Child*. Harmondsworth: Penguin Books.

Schur, E. (1971) *Labeling Deviant Behaviour*. New York: Harper & Row.

Schur, E. (1980) *The Politics of Deviance*. Englewood Cliffs: Prentice Hall.

Sebald, H. (1968) *Adolescence*, Englewood Cliffs: Prentice Hall.

Sellin, T. (1938) *Culture Conflict and Crime*. New York: Social Science Research Council.

Shanley, F. (1966) The Aggressive Middle Class Delinquent. *Journal of Criminal Law, Criminology and Police Science* 57: 145–51.

Sheldon, W. (1949) *Varieties of Delinquent Youth*. New York: Harper & Bros.

Simmel, G. (1969) The Metropolis and Mental Life. In Sennett, R. (ed.) *Classic Essays on the Culture of Cities*. New York: Appleton-Century-Crofts.

Simmon, G. and Trout, G. (1967) Hippies in College – From Teeny-Boppers to Drug Freaks. *Transaction* 5: 27–32.

Smart, C. (1976) *Women, Crime and Criminology*. London: Routledge & Kegan Paul.

Suchar, C. (1978) *Social Deviance*. New York: Holt, Rinehart & Winston.

Sutherland, E. (1939) *Principles of Criminology*. Philadelphia: Lippincott.

Tannenbaum, F. (1938) *Crime and Community*. New York: Ginn.

Taylor, I., Walton, P., and Young, J. (1973) *The New Criminology*. London: Routledge & Kegan Paul.

Taylor, I., Walton, P., and Young, J. (1975) *Critical Criminology*. London: Routledge & Kegan Paul.

Thomas, W. (1923) *The Unadjusted Girl*. Boston: Little Brown.

Tittle, C. (1975) Labelling and Crime: An Empirical Investigation. In W. Gove (ed.) *The Labelling of Deviance*. New York: Halstead.

Toner, B. (1982) *The Facts of Rape*. London: Arrow Books.

Turk, A. (1969) *Criminality and the Legal Order*. Chicago: Rand McNally.

Vold, G. (1958) *Theoretical Criminology*. New York: Oxford University Press.

116

Weyer, E.M. (1924) *The Eskimos*. New Haven: Yale University Press.

Wilson, E. (1983) *What is to be Done about Violence Against Women?* Harmondsworth: Penguin Books.

Wright, E. (1978) *Class, Crisis and the State*. London: New Left Books.

York, P. (1980) *Style Wars*. London: Sidgwick & Jackson.

Index